PRAISE for *Not the Mother I Remember*

"*Not the Mother I Remember* is two linked sto............................deep desire to understand her mother's extraordinary search for personal freedom and its lasting effect on her own life. Honest, engaging, poignant, and beautifully, elegantly written—a mother-daughter memoir you won't forget."

> — Susan Wittig Albert
> author of *A Wilder Rose*
> and founder of Story Circle Network

"In *Not the Mother I Remember*, Amber Starfire resurrects her childhood and young motherhood as the daughter of an unusually individualistic mother who indulged impulses to explore life on her own terms, sometimes dangerously and always in ways that greatly impacted her children. Using excerpts from her mother's journals and letters, the author juxtaposes her mother's voice with her own memories; in the process, she frees herself from the emotional cage her mother's ideas built, while allowing readers to see that strength often lies not in breaking ties but in examining them, not in answers but in living the questions."

> — Sheila Bender
> founder of WritingItReal.com
> and author of *A New Theology: Turning to Poetry in a Time of Grief and Sorrow* and *Creative Writing DeMystified*

"Amber Lea Starfire takes a gamble when she decides to examine seventy years' worth of her dead mother's letters, notebooks, and diaries. What she uncovers about her enigmatic mother in this achingly honest memoir is often disturbing, but the transformation she undergoes becomes her true legacy. *Not the Mother I Remember* is the story of a modern-day Pandora who opens a box of trouble and sets herself free."

— Susan Bono
editor of *Tiny Lights: A Journal of Personal Narrative*
www.tiny-lights.com

"A standing ovation for Amber Lea Starfire's *Not the Mother I Remember*. In this stunning memoir, Starfire details her complex relationship with her fiercely independent and adventurous mother. Five Stars for this riveting and thought-provoking story."

— Robbi Sommers Bryant
President, Redwood Writers
and author of award winners *Dream* and *The Beautiful Evil*

"Amber Lea Starfire has invented an ingenious approach to exploring a fascinating and complicated mother-daughter relationship. Her memoir is full of power and revelation."

— Frances Lefkowitz
author of *To Have Not: A Memoir*

"With her signature clear eye and her courageous striving toward having a clear heart, too, Amber Lea Starfire tells the story of a mother whose life she knew only from the outside, the child's perspective. The result is a stunning literary feat many of us only dream of attempting: stitching together a parent's journals into story, taking a heroic journey through a past we hope to put to rest—and for good reason. *Not the Mother I Remember is* both universal and deeply unique, a book you won't soon forget."

> — Rebecca Lawton
> author of *Junction, Utah* and
> *Reading Water: Lessons from the River*

NOT THE MOTHER I REMEMBER

NOT THE MOTHER I REMEMBER

A MEMOIR

Amber Lea Starfire

MoonSkye Publishing
NAPA, CA

Book Layout ©2013 BookDesignTemplates.com
Cover Design by Monique Aira Aslarona

Not the Mother I Remember/ Amber Lea Starfire.
ISBN: 978-0-9848636-3-1

Library of Congress Control Number: 2013921224

MoonSkye Publishing
1351 2nd St. #5562
Napa, CA 94581
www.moonskyepublishing.com

For my mother, Jacquelyn B. Carr
February 22, 1923 – May 6, 2007

Contents

Preface

Story is integral to human nature. Almost from birth, from the moment we are able to use our imaginations, we create stories to make sense of our experiences and of life in general. These stories become the basis of our personal identities and world views. We then attach the stories to images and store them in memory. And while our memory-stories embody truths about how we perceive people and experiences, our stories, like funhouse mirrors, reflect images distorted by youth, immaturity, and layers of earlier stories. When we write or talk about our most important relationships—those with our parents—we can't help but project distorted images into the world.

How can we know the truth of our relationships when we know only one side of the story? Most people never have an opportunity to know their parents' inner stories, peer at the world through their parents' eyes, or understand how their parents see themselves. But after my mother's death in 2007, when I uncovered boxes containing more than seventy years' worth of her letters and journal entries, I realized I had been given an opportunity for a less distorted view of our troubled relationship.

Not the Mother I Remember is a memoir about my life with Jackie Carr. In these pages, I attempt to portray our disparate world views, while simultaneously chronicling my emotional and intellectual journey as I delve into her writing.

In a broad sense, this story is about the universal themes of mother-daughter bonding, conflict, loss, and love, and what it is like to be a sensitive girl raised by an extraordinarily unconventional woman during a time of social upheaval. But it is also the story of an adult daughter's journey through her mother's life, from her mother's point of view, and how that journey affects and transforms her own narrative.

When I began, I hoped that by comparing my memories with Jackie's recounting of events I might find the truth somewhere between our different versions. But as I read, it became apparent that my mother's life, while parallel to mine in time, did not parallel mine in experience; she rarely touched on events significant to my story. Over the forty-four-year span of this memoir, there were only six[1] of these moments.

Not the Mother I Remember weaves together three narrative strands: 1) my younger self, relating the stories of memory; 2) my adult self, relating my discoveries and reflections as I read my mother's accounts; and 3) Jackie's points of view as recorded in her writing.

As with all stories that rely on memory, I have made a concerted effort to portray events and people as truthfully and accurately as possible. Others may remember them differently, but these are the true stories of my memories. To better convey the impact of certain events on my life, some events have been compressed into a single scene. Some minor characters have been given pseudonyms and, as is the case with all memoir, dialogue is an approximation.

The sections titled "Jackie" may raise the most questions in the reader's mind, so I explain here how I reconstructed her voice:

- I gathered excerpts from her letters that relate to the narrative or issues raised by the memories of my younger self.
- Though arranged as if written in one letter, each Jackie section is comprised of excerpts written by Jackie during the same time pe-

---

[1] These scenes are recorded in "Sabbatical," "Summer Flight," and "Sex Education."

riod as my stories, or written later in Jackie's life *about* that period. In most cases, I kept the excerpts in the order written, except where rearrangement provided a stronger flow and strengthened Jackie's intended meaning.

- Most excerpts are stories, opinions, and viewpoints Jackie expressed many times in letters to multiple people, or in journal entries. Her intended meaning was made clear through repetition.

- To focus Jackie's voice, I changed the recipient of all her writing to "you," as if intended for me. Doing so does not change substance or meaning. For example, if she wrote, "I was afraid for my children," I edited the text to read, "I was afraid for you children."

- The words and substance are Jackie's. I have edited only for consistency and clarity of meaning, correcting grammar, spelling, and punctuation errors, as well as shifting all entries to past tense.

- For the last three "Jackie" sections (Part Three), I corrected syntax and word choice to give her voice a coherence that was not present in her writing due to advancing Alzheimer's— particularly in the last of her documents, from 2001–2002, in which she made syntax errors, repeated words, and mislabeled objects. To have included her entries verbatim would have shifted the emphasis of those sections from her meaning to the effects of her illness and would have detracted from my intentions for the memoir.

Not the Mother I Remember is divided into a prologue and three parts, arranged in roughly chronological order. Part One begins when I am in my late twenties reflecting on my relationship with my mother. It then moves back in time and covers my early years, from 1963 to mid-1966. Part Two covers my pre-teens to mid-twenties. Part Three begins at the onset of my mother's illness, moves through her death, and ends in the present.

To avoid confusion, it will help for you to know that after my mother's death I changed my name to Amber Lea Starfire. I was given the name Linda Carr at birth and, throughout the memoir, I am referred to as either Linda Carr or Linda Peterson (my married name). The author, Amber Lea Starfire, Linda Carr, and Linda Peterson are all the same person.

In addition to a glimpse into one woman's story of a complicated mother-daughter relationship, I hope reading this memoir will give you insight into your own life stories. And I hope that if your parents are still alive, you will seek to discover how their narratives can intersect and transform yours, giving you greater understanding into the complexity of memory, world view, and story.

Prologue

My brothers stand behind me, silent as shadows, as I unlock and open the door leading from the dreary corridor into our mother's one-bedroom apartment, into those tiny rooms in which she'd closeted herself for so long. We pause in the doorway, held back by something invisible in the familiar, stale air—its peculiar sense of emptiness, a lingering accusation, or maybe a reluctance to face our sadness head-on.

"Well, let's get to it," Mike says finally, propelling his large bulk past me into the living room. David and I follow, the apartment now crowded with moving bodies.

After placing my mother in Ralston Village in Belmont—chosen for its lush gardens, well-equipped Alzheimer's wing, and low staff-to-resident ratio—my younger brothers, Mike and David, and I have come to empty her Santa Clara apartment. On the way, I have been all business, leading them briskly forward, keys jingling in my hand. Anyone seeing us cram into the elevator would never guess that we have the same mother: David, with red hair, freckles, and a round, friendly face, all compact muscle inside his five-foot-nine-inch, stocky Irish frame; Mike, standing six-foot-five, like a giant mountain man fresh from the backwoods, complete with flannel shirt, jeans, untamed hair, and scraggly beard; me, big-boned but average height, with short, straight hair and sharp features, often mistaken for a Midwest conservative.

I am the only one who thought to bring cardboard boxes and garbage bags—not nearly enough, I see at once—and my brothers are looking to me for direction. I gaze around the room, trying to decide where to begin. To be here without my mother, to go through her things and dispose of them while she is still alive, even though she won't have any further use for them, feels wrong. Like vultures circling her remains.

"Start with the bed," I say, handing David a garbage bag.

The daybed she's slept on for fifteen years stands against the living room wall, its orange corduroy coverlet still showing the outline of her body. Each night she'd fold herself inside a blanket and lie on top, her head resting on a satin pillowcase-wrapped cushion. During the day, she'd push the rolled-up blanket behind that same cushion. Bloodstains dot the pillowcase, from the time she fell and later awakened lying on the bathroom floor, head in a pool of blood. She'd wiped up the mess, swallowed an aspirin, and gone to bed, her head on that cushion. The next morning, someone had seen her walking down the street, matted hair seeping blood into the back of her collar, and called an ambulance.

When I showed up at her hospital bedside, she said, "I took care of myself," as proud as a child having dressed herself for the first time, buttons askew and shoes on the wrong feet. That was the first time I understood how frail she'd become. I swallowed hard, mustered a cheerful smile, and told her I was there to take her home.

In spite of my brothers' resistance—they thought our mother would be fine on her own—I decided she needed full-time care.

At first, I tried to keep her in her apartment. It isn't really funny, but I smile now, remembering how I hired caretaker after caretaker and how, after I left each time, Mom threw their suitcases out the door and then locked them out when they ran into the hall to retrieve their belongings. Wily Coyote, my mother. Then, my sister-in-law Cat (Richard's wife) stayed for a while, but when Cat told me she found Mom wandering in the hallway at night dressed in nothing but her underwear,

I felt I had no choice. We had to move her someplace where she could be looked after all the time, someplace with locks on the doors.

And now we are here, dismantling her apartment. Taking apart what remains of her life.

The memories and the dark, airless room close in on me. A claustrophobic panic crawls up my chest into my throat, making it difficult to breathe. As Mike and David stuff the coverlet and cushions into a garbage bag, raising clouds of dead skin cells, I cross the room to where the nicest thing she owns—a sixties-era, walnut dinette set with three chairs—crowds the shuttered and curtained windows. I yank open the curtains, raise the blinds, and crank open the windows. Fresh air floods me with relief, but the light from the window reveals how filthy the place is.

There is little here that anyone in the family will want. The photo albums, framed pictures, and videos, certainly. But Mom had long ago made duplicates and parsed out most of those. For twenty years, she's been systematically ridding herself of valuables, paring down her life until there is nothing left. What she *has* retained is either starkly practical, like the card table supporting her computer, or holds precious memories like the trinkets and postcards she brought back from Sri Lanka. What can loosely be called "furniture" was secondhand to begin with; now, years later, it is mostly fodder for the open-mouthed dumpster behind the apartment building.

As she became ill, my mother had withdrawn into her apartment, refusing to open the blinds as if the world outside had nothing left to offer. The place had developed an odor I can only describe as "old person," a dry, indefinite, off smell, a precursor to decay.

She didn't own a vacuum, preferring to pick up lint by hand or use her old-fashioned rug sweeper. Now, my stomach turns at the sight of the long strands of grey hair glinting on the dirty beige carpet. I don't know which is worse—having had to lock up my own mother or seeing the state in which I'd allowed her to live. For six months before moving her to Ralston Village, I'd occasionally enlisted my brothers to get her out of the apartment so I could clean it, but I never had time to do much more than clean the kitchen and bathroom before she made them bring her home. I had wanted to let her remain free and independent as long as possible, but I'd waited too long. Damned either way, I think.

My brothers, as mismatched in height and strength as the furniture, wrestle the daybed's mattress out the door, down the long hallway, and outside to the waiting dumpster.

A rickety folding shelf made of black plastic-laminated particleboard and gold-colored "wrought iron" holds a few treasured books. I thumb through *The Family of Man,* published in 1955, the year I was born—it was her all-time favorite book of photography—before plunking it into a box along with *The Irish in America,* National Geographic's *The photographs,* and *Spiritual Sayings of Khalil Gibran.*

I scoop doilies and long-dead plants from the dinette—my mother had stabbed fake roses into the pots for their bright, scarlet color—before my brothers carry it downstairs and add it to the Goodwill stack, along with the stained, orange armchair she sat in to watch TV, the TV itself, and the imitation oak entertainment center. I box knick-knacks, doilies, statuettes, picture frames, videos, and picture albums, taping and labeling everything for storage. At some point, I'll go through the boxes, but I can't deal with all this stuff now. Not yet.

Gritting my teeth, I turn to the kitchenette containing a small refrigerator, wall cabinets, a sink, a stove, and two feet of counter space covered by the microwave. I have always thought Mom's kitchen revealed her priorities more than any other room. Ragged-edged paper towels, dried for reuse, lie on top of Styrofoam cups stacked upside down on a shelf. The dingy Styrofoam cups, washed and reused many times, are dented and have lipstick and teeth marks around the edges. Plastic grocery bags filled with more plastic grocery bags, scraps of paper, bits of string, and rubber bands fill the shelf beneath the cups.

Her idiosyncrasies have always been the basis of spirited family jokes on her birthday and Christmas. She used to laugh with us and say that the Reduce, Reuse, and Recycle program had been modeled after her. If anything can be claimed to have been her religion, it is frugality. I push everything disposable into trash bags along with the sour contents of the refrigerator.

The cabinets hold mismatched plastic dishes, silverware, and a few dented pans, all of which go into a box for Goodwill; someone might want them. I can hear my mother's voice as though she stands behind me now commenting on my every action, and I want to do what she would have done.

In the bedroom—her office—stands the card table and computer; a folding chair; a four-drawer file cabinet; a black, cardboard-backed dresser with missing drawer pulls; and an ancient stationary bicycle. Shelves are stacked with papers and boxes of old, floppy computer disks. Comfortable, easy-care polyester clothing from the '70s and '80s fills the closet. There are more pictures and doilies and knick-knacks.

I take down from the wall the family headstone rubbing Mom made at the Woodside Road Cemetery, roll it up, and set it aside. Mom loved the rubbing. She told me that the land had once belonged to the Kreiss side of our family and was, in fact, our family cemetery in the early 1800s. She made the rubbing by wrapping a piece of heavy canvas around a gravestone and rubbing the fabric with colored wax, creating a two-dimensional picture, three feet tall by four feet wide. I have no idea what I'm going to do with it.

I bring up fresh boxes from the car and relieve her filing cabinet of financial records spanning four decades. As I fill each box, I label it and put it aside. Emptying her drawers and closet is harder; I can't let myself feel the full weight of memory and emotion that going through her possessions gives rise to, the uneasy sense that the most important part of her—her essence—has already died.

It's a move, like any move, that's all, I tell myself. I sift through her clothing, costume jewelry, undergarments, and hand-knit sweaters, deciding what to keep, what to throw away, and what goes to Goodwill. What I'm not sure about, I dump into a storage box.

As the afternoon wears on and I become tired, more things fall into the garbage pile. I can't imagine having to do this for a parent with a three-bedroom home and two-car garage, and silently thank my mother for having gotten rid of so much, leaving the odious task more manageable. She's done nearly everything: created a trust and assigned me as trustee with full power of attorney, allowing me to take over without a court order. Yes, she did everything except understand that she would someday be forced to move from her apartment. Can I really blame her for that? It could be so much worse.

I stop when I see the white, sealskin coat at the back of the closet, remembering how she'd modeled it for me after her trip to Alaska with one of her boyfriends. It must have been sometime during the '60s. Joe, was it? Ed? I can't remember. I remember only the sparkle in her eyes as she posed, holding the collar with both hands and twirling around. She'd spent a scandalous $800 for the coat and its matching hat with fur trim, a spontaneous purchase completely out of character for the mother I knew. She'd actually giggled when she showed it to me. But she'd been unable to enjoy the extravagance and had worn it only once, maybe twice, before wrapping it in plastic and putting it away. Now, here it is, tucked in the dark like her memories. The white leather, once soft and supple, is stiff and cracked with age, and I can't help thinking of her mind, as cracked and unusable as this coat.

I shove the coat into a garbage bag and survey the nearly empty apartment. Then, I remember the storage closet. I'd found a keychain with several keys on it in her top dresser drawer; with masking tape, one key had been marked "locker." Picking up the keychain, I trudge down the hall toward the storage room.

The dingy hall is dimly lit, with fading green walls stretching to a lone window, an uncurtained square of filtered light. My pale shadow floats behind me on the worn beige carpet.

A small brass plate marks the fourth door on the left as "Storage." Only one key looks like it will fit. The door opens to reveal a dark room the size of a large walk-in closet. I find a light switch and flip it on. The naked sixty-watt bulb dangling from a high ceiling barely illuminates the space. On each side of a narrow aisle are floor-to-ceiling, unfinished plywood cabinets with hardware store hinges, hasps, and padlocks. Deep in the shadows at the far end, I find the cabinet labeled with Mom's number: 205-E. At first, I think I've got the wrong key, because it won't turn in the padlock, but after I jiggle and twist it back and forth, the lock springs open.

Inside the closet-like cabinet, I see cardboard boxes stacked on top of one another. At least I won't have to box up this stuff—I've run out of boxes. I pull each one out of the cabinet. There's our old Super 8 film camera, the one Dad used to make movies of our birthday parties and beach outings; the home movies stopped after the divorce. There is an old VHS video camera with a boom microphone and blank cassettes; I can barely make out the labels in the feeble light. There are extra copies of books my mother authored: *Learning Is Living, Crisis in Intimacy, Communicating and Relating,* and *Communicating with Myself: a Journal.* I open a red-jacketed copy of *Learning Is Living.* It's dedicated to "The Child of My Winter"; she meant David, born when she was forty-six. Flipping to a random page, I read, "Each generation works out its own goals from ever changing need patterns ... it is useless and destructive for us to try and instill our values, in the form of our own need-satisfaction ... into another generation." Huh, I think, and yet that's exactly what you always tried to do, Mom.

My eyes are straining at the small print, so I slide the book back into the box. How is it that my mother could write these books, helping so many people over the years learn how to listen, how to be empathetic and self-aware, yet fail so miserably with her own children? How could she know so much and so little at the same time?

I tug out a misshapen box, held together by layers of duct tape, and inhale sharply when I see what's inside: letters, notebooks, and diaries from the '30s and '40s. I unearth more boxes of letters to and from my mother. Correspondence between Mom and Jack Carr during World War II. Yellow envelopes labeled by years in my mother's uneven scrawl—1956, 1985, 1991, and so on.

As I work my way through the boxes, I feel elated and incredibly sad. Here in my hands is history—the legacy of one woman's experiences and view of life. Perhaps more than one life, if you count all the letters written *to* Jackie. A life now reduced to pages stuffed into dusty boxes and locked away in a dark room.

"You guys don't mind if I keep all these boxes of old letters, do you?" I ask Mike and David, when they come searching for me. I say it casually, but my heart is thumping hard against my ribcage. I will fight for the boxes if either of them objects. But David shrugs and Mike says no, he doesn't mind.

They are *mine.*

As a little girl I loved my mother wholly, but later, when she launched into an all-consuming journey of self-discovery, I felt deserted and rudderless. "Finding yourself" was part of the times, the '60s and '70s, but that's no consolation to me now. It never was.

In these boxes, I wonder, will I find justification for my pain and anger and loss? Will what she's written match what I remember, or will I discover that I've been wrong? I am hungry to find out how she wrote about herself, how she wrote about me, and where I fit into her life. The unexpected possibility of discovering, of coming to understand, of forgiving my mother causes me to tremble.

Then another question occurs to me: if I find here the mother I thought I'd lost, will that discovery heal me? Will it be enough to resolve my inner conflict with her? Will I finally be able to let go of my disappointment and anger, and love her for who she was, or will I still long for the mother I believed she should have been?

Someday, I'll find out. Not yet. It's too much, and I'm not sure I can bear to know her. Not yet, but soon.

PART ONE

Destructive Distillation

I was twenty-seven when I discovered I hated my mother. It happened while I was lying in bed, trying to sleep, husband snoring loudly next to me (this was before our love had spread too thin and brittle to sustain us). After a vain attempt at rousing him, I braced my back against the wall and with my hands and feet rolled him onto his side, where he snorted once or twice and then abruptly, blissfully, stopped. I rolled back onto my pillow and faced the dormer ceiling, which sloped towards my feet and head.

I'd always loved dormers—they reminded me of deliciously secret childhood hiding places—and had tucked our bed, a double mattress and box springs, on the floor under the window, where it fit perfectly. Then I'd claimed the window side of the bed.

The dormer window faced the front of our house, which stood at the top and middle of a T-intersection. If I propped myself up a little, as I did now, I could see down the length of Borthwick Street, the long stem of the "T." Portland's city lights, reflected in a steely, overcast sky, illuminated the houses and lawns as radiantly as a full moon. Amber puddles of light pooling under the street lamps seemed redundant in the face of such a bright night. Except for the occasional bark of a dog, it was quiet. I took all this in while my mind reflected on the events of the day: my battles to get my six- and four-year-old sons to behave, and my phone conversation—argument, rather—with my mother.

It was always the same: two completely different views of one event.

"Yes, I do expect something in return from you," she'd said in response to my saying I didn't owe her anything. Followed by a stream of words, "... your perception ... in denial ... guilty ... angry ... adolescent rebellion ... you owe me." Owe. Obligation.

Shit. I was reliving it again, along with all the things I wished I'd said or should have said and didn't. It wouldn't have mattered anyway. My opinions and feelings meant little to my mother. "Your perception"— magic words that, because the perception was mine, automatically made it wrong. There was never anything I could say to make a difference, short of agreeing with her and doing whatever she requested. End of argument.

I didn't want to think about it. I wanted her out of my head. "Shut UP!" I shouted in my mind. "Can't you just leave me alone?" I turned over angrily and faced the wall, put my hands over my ears, and squeezed my eyes shut. When that didn't work, I sighed and turned onto my back again, helpless. She was right about one thing—with her, I was still, and would always be, an adolescent, petulant and defensive. No matter that I was married and had two children of my own, or that I worked part-time and was respected by my peers. I wished I could run away. But how do you run away from a voice in your head?

That's when I saw it—there, in my heart, and in my gut. It wasn't physical, not something you could see on the outside. But I saw it clearly, as though my eyes could peel back layers of flesh: a black, viscous substance filled the cavernous area inside my ribs. It glooped and bubbled in great, slow craters, like the cooling but still active lava bed I'd seen once in Hawaii. A substance so thick and gelatinous, that if I could have reached in to touch it, I would have stuck fast like Brer Rabbit to the tar baby.

What *was* it?

Then I understood: this pulsing, slow-boiling, tar-like blackness was hatred for my mother. It *burned* in me. Guilt and revulsion swiftly followed this realization. How could I hate my mother? She wasn't a bad woman. She had her faults, but she was only trying to help me in her own way. As a born-again Christian, I wasn't supposed to hate anyone, let alone my mother. Yet even as one part of me backed away from the dark mass, another part wanted to give myself over to it, to bury myself in it. Suffocate. The thought was satisfyingly bleak.

Suddenly nauseated, I felt desperate to purge myself of the horrid thing. But it wasn't something I could just wish away. When had it arrived? How long had it been there? I had known I was angry; I hadn't known my anger was only the visible edge of something grotesque.

I groaned and twisted to my side, pulling the blankets with me. Now I would never get to sleep. I threw back the covers, crawled over my husband's sleeping form, staggered into the bathroom, and shut the door. There I sat on the toilet seat and sobbed tears of frustration, fear, guilt—and hatred. Why, I wondered, did I hate my mother so much?

I hated her for having affairs and for divorcing my father.

I hated her for putting her quest for self-growth and discovery before my emotional needs, and for pushing me out of the house when I was fifteen, unready for the world.

I hated her for her constant criticism, for expecting me to control my husband and children as though they were puppets, and because, in spite of myself, I cared what she thought of me.

I hated her for always one-upping me: whatever trouble I had, she'd had more; however hard I worked or tired I was, she had worked harder and been more tired; whatever I achieved, she'd achieved more and against greater odds.

I hated her for using guilt to control me and then using my own guilt against me, as in, "You're only angry (insert resentful, upset, or resisting) because you feel guilty."

I hated her for using money as a leverage to manipulate me, and I hated myself for letting her do it.

Hate and anger—I tallied the wrongs. And when I was done thinking and crying, I crept back to bed, pulled my hatred over me like a warm blanket, and slept.

In the days and months and years that followed, I became intensely aware of the Tar (as I named it) at certain times: when I thought or spoke about my mother, when I had to deal with her directly, or when my husband accused me of being like her (which was often). But also when I doubted myself, when I tried too hard to please someone—anyone—or when I failed to accomplish something—anything.

I wrote about the Tar in my journal and—once—tried to describe it to my husband. He was uninterested. I never told anyone else about my hatred, judging it unchristian and unseemly. I tried to ignore it, deny it, make it disappear, burnt the journal in which I'd written about it. But the Tar remained.

Sometimes, when my mother let me know I had failed her in some way, it sat soft and heavy in me, like a great bag of crude oil, the weight of it pressing on my lungs so that I could not breathe. Sometimes, when she pushed me too hard, it cooled and solidified and shone like brightly polished obsidian, with painfully sharp edges. And during those times we tried to make up with each other, it became watery and brown, weak as tea. But it was always there in one form or another, and it would be years before anything like compassion or forgiveness would begin to dissolve it.

Tar can be dangerous. If you fall into a tar pit, you might get trapped, suffocate, or starve to death. But tar can also be a healing salve. I used to spread a tar-based ointment on my son's hands to ease the symptoms of psoriasis—sore, cracked, and bleeding skin. Likewise, hatred can be dangerous. If you immerse yourself in it, it can eat you alive. But it may also be used to cover and seal wounds, protecting you from further hurt. When my mother and I were tolerating each other, the Tar was soft and warm and pliable. Spread evenly over sore spots, it soothed and consoled. And so, the Tar dwelling in me would by turns hurt and heal, corrode and soothe.

How had I gone from the little girl who adored her mother—once writing in a fifth-grade essay that I wanted to be exactly like her when I grew up—to feeling such aversion that I could not stand being in her presence or hearing her voice? The Tar, independent and uncontrollable, somehow coexisted in me with that little girl, who never stopped wanting her mother's love and approval, and wanted desperately to love her mother in return.

I was ashamed of my hatred, which—paired with my fear of becoming like her—was deep and wide. Even thirty years later, and more than four years after she passed away, I would feel the bite of that shame. When I thought about her my stomach would clench, trying to purge itself of the thick, dark substance. I often deceived myself to think it went away, but there it would be, once again—a lump of sadness, a heavy chunk of coal—lying hard and cold, in the bottom of my heart.

Shortly after my oldest son's birth in 1976 and approximately six years before the Tar made itself known to me, my mother decided to give forty redwood-forested acres she owned to her children. She called to tell me about it.

"I want to give the La Honda property jointly to all six of you kids. You won't be able to subdivide or sell any part of it, except to your brothers and vice versa."

But I said, "Oh no. I'm not interested in something that involves my brothers. I can't imagine all of us coming to an agreement about *anything*." So she put the property in the names of my five brothers and gave me my share in cash, which my husband and I used to buy five acres in Brush Prairie, Washington. We moved a mobile home onto the land, and it was there I gave birth to my second son. A year after we bought it, we sold the land for twice what we paid for it and used the money for a down payment on a house in nearby Vancouver.

Then, my mother had an annuity pay out shares to each of her six children; the annuity would last six years. She told me she wanted to give her children their inheritance before she died. She wanted to ensure our financial security, she said, as well as beat the IRS by avoiding inheritance taxes. The money comprised a large part of our mortgage payment, enabling me to stay home with my children. I felt grateful and took her gifts at face value. But money is a messy substance and always complicates difficult relationships.

It was my husband's idea to bring together under one roof the members of our Christian band. I was not enthusiastic (we'd lived in a commune on the coast of Oregon for two years before having children), but he could be persuasive and I eventually came around. He also convinced my mother to facilitate his dream (now our dream) and to put up the money for a huge, Victorian-era house—a derelict, ex-halfway-house—on Marshall Street in Northwest Portland. In our proposal, my mother would pay him to convert the building to apartments, which we would manage. I would keep the books. We would all win—she, with monthly rental income and increased equity in the property, we with extra income and a place for our group.

Had any of us been wiser or looked carefully at the plan, we would have seen its glaring faults: my mother, a self-professed penny-pincher, was unwilling to pay for quality work or materials; my husband, who had a full-time day job, didn't have the carpentry, plumbing, or wiring skills to perform the work to code; and I was already over my head raising two children under five while working part-time, playing in the band, and giving flute lessons on the side. Now I added stripping paint from wood molding, removing wallpaper, sanding and repairing plaster walls, refinishing floors, and bookkeeping to the mix. At about the same time, my mother bought a house in Portland for my brother Richard, his wife, and three daughters. I acted as my mother's agent, working with the real estate company to seal the deal. So, in her mind, I became responsible for both houses.

Fast forward through a year of poorly executed renovations; through my drug-addicted brother burning down his house and ending up in rehab; through our band breaking up; through high vacancy rates and financial losses for my mother; through hot arguments and unfair, barbed accusations thrown from both sides; through my dogmatic diatribes against her lifestyle ("Your money won't protect you from Hell!"); through the letter from my mother totaling the value of everything she'd ever given me, including birthday and wedding gifts—with interest added. When I offered to pay her back, she countered that even if I were able to repay the money, which she doubted, I could never repay the time and love and trouble she'd gone through for me. Translation: "You will always owe me." Continue forward through my declaring, "I won't take any more," moving out of the Marshall Street house, and spending months trying to help her sell it—frustrated, because she refused to list it with a real estate agent. Keep moving forward, through my mother lease-optioning the building to a guy who trashed and abandoned the place, leaving it littered with thousands of pornographic Polaroids, all the way to the moment, ten months later, when the house had been condemned by the City—and I, looking out my little dormer window, feeling the blame for everything, became aware of the Tar for the very first time.

Three years later, I sat on a small couch in my North Amsterdam living room, holding the thin leaf of my mother's letter between my trembling fingers. Tears coursed down my cheeks. I wiped my face with the back of one hand, succeeding in nothing more than spreading the salty wetness across my skin. The Tar, which had hardened in the months before we left the U.S., and which had since softened with the physical distance between us, now felt dirty and grossly heavy, a burden I wished to lay down and leave behind.

"I often get choked up when I read your newsletters," she had written. "Any sensitive person can read between the lines. ...the emotional crises that must have accompanied the changes taking place. The tendency to say, 'Everything's fine' is so much easier than the truth. Can you tell me what's going on? I worry about you."

Two years after the Marshall Street fiasco, my husband, Eric, and I had sold our house and, with another couple with whom we played music, took our families to Amsterdam to join Youth With a Mission (YWAM). For a year, we subsisted on donations from church and family members, and every month I wrote a glowing newsletter updating donors about our "successful mission" in Holland. But that was a lie.

Of all the people I knew, of all the people to whom I felt close, of all the people I had counted as family—and my mother had not been one of them—she had been the only one to read the silent distress between the lines of my cheery newsletters.

How had this woman who, I was convinced, had no sensitivity to my thoughts or feelings somehow divined we were in trouble? I took out a copy of my recent newsletter and saw nothing negative in what I'd written. With all the troubles my mother had been going through in the months since we'd left, how had she intuited my situation from so far away? I knew she was still dealing with fallout from the Burnside and Marshall Street properties in Portland, my little brother David had been arrested for burglary and sentenced to juvenile hall, and she was paying for his, as well as two of my other brothers' (Mike and Richard) drug-related legal defenses. She was sixty-two, soon to retire from her teaching position at Foothill College, and had health problems that might require surgery. But she had seen past all of that to me, thousands of miles and an ocean away. For the first time, I began to think of her as real—frail, imperfect, human—and to feel remorse for my attitude towards her.

I looked around our apartment, furnished with a mix of cast-off furniture, Ikea shelving and kitchen items, and homemade wall art in primary colors. In Holland, when you rent an apartment it comes with bare concrete walls and floors, no lighting fixtures, wall outlets or switches, no kitchen cabinets or sinks. Only a toilet in the bathroom. When the previous tenants leave, they're required to remove any carpeting, wallpaper, and fixtures they installed. We'd been lucky to find an apartment where the previous renters were willing to sell us the carpet, the bathtub, kitchen cabinets, and lighting fixtures. Furthermore, they'd agreed to leave the walls painted and wallpapered—for a price. We'd had to add everything else. It had taken six months of scrimping and creativity to get the apartment to the point it was. We'd begun to feel relatively comfortable, but it was still far from feeling like home.

That night, I locked myself in my bedroom and called her. It was 7:00 a.m. in Palo Alto. "Mom?" I cried on the phone. "It's been awful, really awful."

"What's happened?" she said.

"Right after we arrived, YWAM put us through eight weeks of training ... to make us obedient, you know? It was sitting in classrooms eight hours a day, being told what to think. We weren't allowed to go to the bathroom when we needed to, or see our kids, except in the evenings."

"How could you put up with that?"

"I don't know. I was confused. I wanted to serve God ... figured they knew better than I did ... I guess it all worked on me. But you know how nonconformist Eric is. He refused to 'behave,' so they punished us. Me too, though I had done everything they told me." I paused, picturing the crowded little classroom and the stern faces of our instructors.

Static crackled between us. "Go on," she said.

"They broke up the band and separated us from the others. I made it sound like it was our choice in the newsletters, but it wasn't. We weren't allowed to play our music—not even for church services. We had sessions where they tried to break Eric down. The pressure was horrible. No one would talk to us. I had something like a nervous breakdown. Locked myself in my bedroom and screamed for two hours. It was like falling off a cliff into darkness."

"Oh, Linda," she said. I could hear the concern in her voice. "Why didn't you call?"

"I was just coping, trying so hard to do what I was supposed to. Later, after everything calmed down, they gave us our duties. I've been working as a secretary in the main office, and they gave Eric a hammer and put him in the basement, as a carpenter. I just kept hoping that things would get better, that we'd get to do what we came here to do. But the boys have suffered, too... daily bullying and beatings in the Dutch schools. Evan's so big, he stands up for himself pretty well. But poor Ezra... he's had it the worst. I finally had to tell him to fight back."

I started to cry again.

"And now... Mom?... we just found out that the mutual fund where we invested the money from our house was a fraud. It's gone—all of it—along with millions of other investors' dollars. We weren't the only ones," I rushed to say. I wanted her to know that even experienced investors had been duped. "The FBI says there's little chance of ever recovering it. We can't even buy tickets to come home. I don't know what to do." A heavy sense of failure weighed down on my chest, crushing the breath out of me.

"Linda, you know me better than that," she said. "How much do you need?"

I grabbed a tissue, wiped my face, tried to calm myself. She waited until I could speak. "You know I don't want to ask... God, I hate this! Just enough for plane tickets and maybe a place to stay for a couple of months. Until we can get on our feet again."

My mother sent the money for our plane tickets and offered to loan us the down payment on another house. I refused, wanting to avoid taking more money from her than I had to. So she gave us a room in her house—sacrificing treasured privacy—until we could find jobs and save enough to rent a place.

Within a few weeks of returning to California, I found a secretarial job. I would come home from a long day of work, tired and dispirited, feeling lost in life. (Looking back now, I realize I was seriously depressed.) My mother would greet me at the door. "Linda, those boys made a mess in my kitchen again. You've got to get them to clean up after themselves. And they do nothing but fight. Today, I had to tear them off each other. And that husband of yours ... he mopes around doing nothing. He could be helping. I have a whole list of things that need fixing around here ..."

"Mom, just let me put my stuff down, okay? I'm tired and need a little space."

"You get nothing *but* space. When I was your age, I had four children and managed a hotel while Jack worked. Then I went to school in the evenings. And he worked as hard as I did. We were like clockwork; he would make one side of the bed while I made the other. Eric is nothing but a weight around your ankles."

"Okay, Mom. What do you need me to do? And where's Eric?"

"I want you to get the boys to clean up their mess. And if you could get Eric to change that light bulb when he gets home ... he's out doing something, I don't know." She'd roll her eyes with exaggerated disgust, "and then get him to fix the bookshelf in my office ... it's breaking down. You'd think, with all that I do for your family, that he'd be in here offering."

"Just let me change my clothes, okay?"

"You need to do some shopping, too. We're running out of eggs."

I'd go into the bedroom where the four of us slept—the boys in the bunk bed Eric made of two-by-fours and our double mattress on the floor—strewn with dirty clothes and boys' underwear, and change my clothes. Then I'd trudge outside and shout for the boys, who'd be playing in the backyard or somewhere close by. I'd make them pick up their things in the living room and kitchen. I'd ask Eric to change the light bulb and fix the bookcase. I'd ask how the job hunting went. He'd shrug and then play ball in the backyard with the boys while I made dinner, and my mother would be in her office typing letters to everyone telling how much trouble we were and how much she missed her privacy.

Tar is created through destructive distillation: organic material, such as pine or peat or coal, is heated to an extremely high temperature in the absence of air and steam or solvents, until the matter's molecules break down into a complex mixture of compounds.

My Tar must have been formed through some such destructive distillation process: take the natural, organic love that a child feels toward her mother and heat it to extremely high temperatures with divorce, loss of father, and lack of mother's attentions; unsettle with travel, moves to new neighborhoods and schools, brothers leaving home, and a child's misunderstanding of the world; remove the oxygen of guidance, and don't give any kind of breathing room; make sure to demand love's natural actions—time, consideration, phone calls, letters, visits, and a listening ear—while talking only about oneself. Add the pressure of self-absorption until love's molecules break into pieces and form complex compounds—hurt, anger, and finally, hatred.

When pine or coal become tar, are they still also pine or coal? When love becomes anger and hatred, is it still, also, love?

My Tar wasn't complete or pure; what is hatred anyway, if not the complex product of love and pain, desire and blame? The Tar of my hatred was mixed with love, for I loved my mother, too.

I loved her for holding and rocking and nurturing me when I was a baby.

I loved her for making me feel special when I was a little girl, telling me I was beautiful and brilliant, giving me travel experiences, dance and music lessons, and encouraging me to write.

I loved her for dropping everything and coming to Portland to help me after the birth of my first child, traveling to Washington after the birth of my second, and for going out of her way to be an actively engaged grandmother.

I loved her for helping me financially, giving me her used cars and money to buy my first piece of property.

I loved her because even when I hated her, she loved me anyway, rescuing my family from Europe and giving up her own space for us.

Over time, I began to see the Tar not as protection and salve, but as a barrier. I had thought of it as something separate and outside my will—within me, not of me—and necessary as an impenetrable line between where my mother ended and I began. Something to keep me from *becoming* her. In reality, I had been keeping the Tar alive, nourishing it with blame and resentment. It was time to purge.

There are several ways to remove tar; all of them involve solvents, most are flammable, poisonous and cause irritation if they come into contact with the skin: lighter fluid, kerosene, lacquer thinner, mineral spirits, and gasoline. Concentrated citrus cleaners will also dissolve tar—safer, but still skin irritating. Every method requires time and lots of elbow grease. First, you use a paint scraper, or similar tool, to scoop out or scrape off as much of the black goop as possible. Then, you apply a solvent and gently scrub with a brush. For the remaining, stubborn bits of tar, spray on the solvent and let sit for a few minutes. Scrub again. When all of the tar is removed, you need to cleanse the entire area with a gentle mixture of detergent and water, then rinse. Using this process, you should be able to remove most, if not all, of the tar.

Over the years, I worked hard at removing my Tar. All the solvents were irritating, some of them flammable. I scooped out the greatest mass of Tar with the sharp tools of gratitude and honest reflection, and smeared it onto the pages of my journals. The Tar appeared dense and ugly in the light. And when I eventually burnt the journals, the flames seemed to reach higher and burn hotter than normal, fed by the pitch of acknowledged hatred.

Then, the solvent—a mixture of acceptance and forgiveness—had to be applied to those traits of my mother's I had internalized or inherited or adopted: self-absorption; a need to be "right" and blame others when things go wrong; a drive to achieve, which keeps my fingers always busy knitting, crafting, typing, and multi-tasking; talking too much and listening too little; trusting others to a fault; and trying to be too much in control of life. Only after the difficult process of scrubbing through layers of accumulated judgment could my healing begin. Only after letting the solvent sit for a while, giving it a chance to break down the resisting surface compounds.

The great irony is that even as I worked at scrubbing away the Tar, my mother was fading away, a victim of Alzheimer's disease. As time went on, I visited her more often and tried to listen to—rather than tune out—her oft-repeated stories. I did her grocery shopping and ran small errands for her. We went on walks together. But as she slipped into the dark isolation of dementia, she began to view me as the enemy. I was the one who took her car keys away, who sent people to check up on her each day, who threw out moldy food from the refrigerator when she wasn't looking. And, though I wasn't the one who actually drove her to the assisted living facility, she understood that I had made the decision to put her there. I represented the loss of her freedom, and she would never forgive that, even when she no longer remembered why she hated me. We had changed places, my mother and I; the Tar had found a new home.

Dissolution of an All-American Family

When I cleaned out my mother's apartment, I kept only a few things: a couple of paintings she had loved, the three-foot-tall Kuan Yin statue, her photo albums, financial records, and the boxes I discovered containing her letters and journals. At the time, I had been too heartsick over her illness and too busy with her care to deal with any of it, so I stashed it all in a rented storage room. For later.

Now, three years after her death, I roll open the storage door and peer into the room's cool shadows, the afternoon sun warm on my back, waiting for my eyes to adjust. There, on the left—past the stacks of photography supplies, books, photo albums, and boxes filled with old clothing and Halloween costumes—my mother's stuff.

Reaching up, I grab a box that appears to be constructed entirely of duct tape, heft it down from its shelf, and slit it open with a box knife. Ten or twelve ragged manila envelopes lie side by side, each one with a year and a list of key events scrawled in my mother's uneven handwriting on the back of it. I flip through them: 1989, 1992, 1974, 1955—the year of my birth.

These boxes of envelopes, chalked with dust and weathered soft from age, seem to hold not only my mother's memories but also the shadows and edges of my own. So here I am, sitting on a cold cement floor, rummaging through my mother's papers because I can't seem to shake the idea that somewhere between our two versions of life I'll find the truth.

Another box contains my mother's and father's wartime letters. Pages filled with *swells* and *goshes* and *oh boys*—language from a time so relatively innocent I find it comical and touching. She used to tell me, "I married Jack because I knew he would let me make all the decisions. I knew I could control him." I believed her, because that's how I knew her to be. Still, I have a hard time imagining any twenty-year-old calculating her life so carefully, so unemotionally. These letters, filled with words evident of simpler times, seem to challenge her account, and I am beginning to doubt that my mother was as shrewd as she had led me to believe. I put the box of letters aside and continue to rummage, not sure exactly what I'm searching for.

Then I find a small, mahogany leather diary, slightly larger than the palm of my hand, huddled among some loose papers. When I pull it out and see "1963" scribbled in red ink on the first page, my heart quickens. I always blamed Mom for my parents' divorce and Dad's leaving, but I was only eight at the time; I remember—at best—a muddled and conflicting mix of events. Here is a chance to find out what really happened, at least from my mother's perspective. The tiny, leather-bound diary, my key to the past, seems to shimmer with promise.

When I finally roll down the door to the storage unit, it is that diary and two manila envelopes labeled "1963" and "1964" that I carry home.

I don't read the diary right away. In my hands, the worn leather cover is pliable and smooth, and the book feels fat, heavier than it should for its size. I suspect my mind is playing tricks, imparting physical weight to the diary's emotional significance, which makes me think about the difference between appearance and reality—and my mind goes back in time, to 1959 and our move to the house in San Mateo.

Even before our bags were unpacked, before my dad and older brothers had finished hauling our belongings out of the moving truck, I had raced across the street to where I'd seen another little girl my age playing in her yard. I halted on the sidewalk bordering her lawn, suddenly shy, hands clasped behind my back. When she looked up from her solitary game of jacks I blurted, "Do you want to be my friend?" She nodded, and that's how I made my first best friend at the age of four. And though my family would live in that house on the corner of Yew Street fewer than six years, it's the place I always name when someone asks, "Where did you grow up?"

We moved there because my mother had gotten a job teaching high school English at Hillsdale High School, only a mile away. I didn't know where Dad worked, but I knew he was a mechanic and that he knew everything there was to know about cars. There were five of us children: four boys and a girl. Terry, John, Richard, and I were born four years apart, in that order, until my parents broke the pattern with my little brother Michael who arrived only twenty-two months after I did.

I loved the sturdy, white, colonial-style house, which seemed to anchor the corner to the foot of the hill, its window-eyes watching over the quiet neighborhood like a sentinel. Cheerful red brick steps led up to the wide, four-pillared porch and to the door, which, with a houseful of children banging in and out of it, would always be open.

The first time you walked through that front door, you'd find yourself in an open entryway with a large living room on the left—perfect for building elaborate card pavilions, playing games of tag, or bowling with marbles. The formal dining room, used only for parties and holiday dinners, was on the right. Straight ahead, the stairs beckoned upward to the second floor.

Up the beige-carpeted stairs to the second-floor landing, the first bedroom to the left was Richard's, with the two large fish tanks that housed his garter snakes. I helped him hose the snakes out of their underground dens in the yard, where he captured and made them into pets. Sometimes he charged the neighborhood boys 50 cents to watch one of the snakes swallow a mouse whole, and I'd loiter at the edge of the crowd of boys, as fascinated by their shoving and gleeful shouts and "eeews" as they were with the morbid process of feeding.

On the other side of the landing was the upstairs hallway, separated from the stairs by a waist-high banister. Then John's room, which he shared with Terry, who was away at college. My bedroom was at the next corner, facing the front of the house and directly across the hall from my parents' room. Mike slept in a tiny room between us that might have been a sewing room or a large closet at one time. Tight quarters, but at least he didn't have to share.

My room was my sanctuary, the one place I could escape the noise and violent roughhousing of my brothers. I loved its pink walls, which were not one color, but bloomed and faded from a deep blush to a light pastel, so that I imagined I lived in the heart of a rose. Through its windows, I looked out over the expanse of the front lawn, dotted with crabapple and peach trees, sloping gently down to the massive oak on the corner and the street beyond. I spent hours in this room, playing with my dolls or reading tales of princesses and knights.

Outside, the fruit trees and berry vines surrounding the house flourished in the mild climate of the San Francisco peninsula. We picked fruit year round. I loved plucking ripe figs from their leafy branches, or climbing into the branches of the cherry tree, eating its tart red fruit and spying on the neighbors.

I remember those early days as a euphoria of freedom and discovery. Mike, Richard, and I roamed for miles unattended and played typical childhood games with our neighborhood friends: School (I insisted on being the teacher), or War (I fought with my brothers over the role of

General), or Pirates (I usually ended up walking the plank). We made tunnels in the tall grass across the street, constructed forts, and collected caterpillars. We never had to ask permission for anything. At mealtimes, someone would stand on the stoop outside the front door, cup his hands on the side of his mouth, and bellow a long-winded "Dinnnner!" to call us in. Had we been on a farm instead of on the edge of the suburbs (there was a horse ranch and stables at the end of our dead-end street), we might have used a triangle to announce meals.

An old, corrugated metal shed squatted in our backyard. The previous owners had boarded a horse in it; we used it as a henhouse. When we wanted eggs, we collected them. When chicken was on the menu, my father would catch one and chop off its head. We children would watch, fascinated, as the headless bird flopped around the yard in a wild, macabre dance, blood spurting everywhere. Then my mother scalded, plucked, cleaned, and prepared it for the dinner that we'd eat together at the Formica kitchen table.

Richard and Mike and I, the three youngest, used to crawl into our parents' warm bed on weekend mornings, forcing my sleepy mother and father to the edges, where they would give way and roll out the sides of the bed. Then, my mother would make pancakes or French toast or waffles for breakfast, except on Easter, when we would have creamed egg on toast.

On the surface, except for the fact that my mother was not a stay-at-home mom, we were the stereotypical "Ozzie and Harriet," "Leave It to Beaver" kind of family. That is, we were a solid, middle class family with five rowdy, happy kids and two working parents. For the most part, we played our roles: my mother kept the house clean, did the laundry, and cooked the meals; my father maintained the yard and the cars, kept the movie camera rolling during birthday parties, and fell asleep in front of the TV after dinner; and my brothers tormented each other and me as much as possible.

The world was wide and solid beneath our feet.

My mother was vivacious and smart, and when she laughed, her chin tilted upward and her eyes lit her entire face. When I was seven, she took me with her to work one day. She told me to sit at the back of the classroom and be quiet. Each period, a bell rang, the room would empty, and thirty new students would rush in, chattering like flocks of birds. Mom sat on the edge of her desk, one leg planted firmly on the floor, as she opened a paperback and began reading to her students. When she was done, she moved around the room asking questions: "Who is the protagonist in this story? Who is the antagonist? Where is the conflict in this passage?"

It was obvious that my mother was a good teacher. Her students liked her, and I understood why: she treated them with respect, as though they weren't just kids. She gave them the power to choose what books they wanted to read and helped them develop learning plans and grade their own work—radical ideas at the time. Watching her that day, my heart swelled with pride. I knew when I grew up I would be a teacher, just like her, and I would get married and have five children, just like her—only I would have three boys and two girls, instead of four boys and one girl, because a girl should have a sister.

But Mom started coming home later and later after school, and she would leave again in the evening: meetings, classes, high school chat sessions. There were weekend workshops and continuing education classes. When she *was* home, it seemed she was always in her office—not actually a separate room, but a divided end of our long living room—fingers flying over the keys of her typewriter. Built-in shelving, filled with books, lined two walls from floor to ceiling. In places, books spilled out onto the floor. When I tried to get her attention, she'd continue typing while absently pretending to listen. And while she wrote, I prattled, running my fingers along the books' spines, reading their titles, and inhaling their special mustiness—a literary perfume I would always associate with books, and with my mother.

She said she loved teaching because she could be home after school and during the summers, when we were also home. But what I remember is my mother's absence and the parade of people who exchanged childcare and gardening services in return for the studio apartment over our garage. There was the sweet, young couple with the fat, dark-haired baby, the skinny Mexican couple who left after the husband cut his thumb off in the lawn mower, and the older woman who seemed to do nothing but yell at us every chance she got. We ran wild and minded none of them. They never stayed long, anyway.

Then, Richard and John had to share a room because we started taking in pregnant teenage girls who attended my mother's after-school counseling sessions. The girls' parents had kicked them out after learning they were pregnant, and Mom wanted to give them a place to stay until they had their babies. Sometimes we had two or three girls at a time. There was Starr, a short, dark-haired girl, who had twins. Kara, so tall and willowy and frail-seeming, even during pregnancy, that I worried about her. There were others whose names I don't remember, and finally Shari, who latched onto my mother as though she were drowning—and stayed latched for the next forty years. To my fascinated eyes, the girls were beautiful and mysterious and alien, secretive and giggling together behind their closed door in the room that used to be Richard's. As their bellies grew rounder, they became moody. They cried and stormed and slammed doors. One day they would fill the house with volatile energy; the next, they'd return from the hospital with red, puffy eyes and flat, flabby stomachs. Then, they'd be gone, and I never knew where they or their babies went.

I could feel tension building in the atmosphere around the house, and especially around my parents. Like the static electricity that causes the hair on your arms and neck to stand away from your skin, and the crackle of electricity before lightning is finally released, we could all feel it.

Late one afternoon, I was in my room playing with my dolls when I heard yelling outside and ran to the window to see what was happening. John, now sixteen, was leaning back against the side of the station wagon, his arms folded in front of him, his expression sullen. I knew he'd started cutting school, taking the family car without permission, and staying out late and drinking on weekends.

Dad yelled something, arms waving in anger. The glass muffled their words, so I couldn't hear what he said, only the high, staccato notes of frustration as he pointed, repeatedly jabbing his finger an inch from John's nose. I saw my mother striding across the lawn to the driveway. And then, everything seemed to happen at once.

John pushed my father's hand away from his face and turned to walk away. My father grabbed his arm, pulling him roughly around. John shoved him, shouting. His face was crimson with rage, making the pimples stand out as bright red dots on cheeks and forehead. Then Dad hit him, full fisted, in the mouth. I gasped and clutched my doll to my chest. Mom screamed and grabbed at Dad's shirt. John fell back, his hand to his mouth, and when it came away, I could see his lips, cut and bloodied by his braces. Dad stood over him, his chest heaving, my mother pulling at his arm and screaming. Finally, Dad turned and trudged back towards the house, his shoulders slumped forward in defeat. Mom went to John, but he pushed her away. Before she could react, he yanked open the car door, jumped in, slammed it shut, and screeched out of the driveway, scraping the station wagon's rear bumper on the street as he left. I saw Mom return to the house, heard the front door slam, and then the loud, angry voices of my parents downstairs.

For a moment, I stood transfixed. Then I lay down on my bed and held my doll against my heart. I stroked her long curls. "It'll be all right," I whispered, wiping tears from my cheeks. Dad never hit us. Mom did sometimes, when one or all of us had pushed her too far, but never Dad. Something awful must have happened to make him so angry. Unpredictable. Changed. Like someone else's dad, not mine. I lay there, scared and trembling and wondering, until I fell asleep. When I woke, the house was quiet.

That summer, John was sent away to Japan to live with the family of an old war buddy of my father's, and Richard had a room to himself again. He'd always been a little mean—Mom said he was jealous of me—but now he was often cruel, and I had to be careful not to be alone with him. He'd pinch me until I cried or grab my chest and make fun of my "itty bitty titties." A few times he captured me, rolled me tightly into a blanket so I couldn't move my arms or legs, and then sat on me, laughing, his weight heavy on my chest. I would cry and struggle until my sweat made the blanket itch against my hot skin. Panicked, I'd sob and beg for him to get off me before I suffocated. But he never let me go until I was completely broken and lying still.

Mike sometimes ganged up on me with Richard. Or he broke things. He pulled the heads off my Barbie dolls and stuck holes in their bodies with pins. My favorite Teddy bear went missing; I found it two months later spray-painted yellow and discarded beneath a bush in the front yard. I was no angel, either. I exacted revenge by going into my brothers' rooms and dumping the contents of their dresser drawers all over the floor, or hiding something they cared about so they couldn't find it. Once I lured Mike, dressed only in his underwear, onto the faux balcony outside his second-floor window, then rushed into his room and locked him out. I stood on my side of the window pointing and laughing at him as he cried and banged on the glass. He was six years old. After a while, we hardly played together anymore.

I have often wondered where my parents were while all this was going on. When I travel back into the shadows of memory, I can't find them. There is only a big, empty house, and I am wandering from room to room, calling their names, hearing only the brush of my soft footsteps against the carpet.

I hardly remember my mother and father together at home. I hardly remember my father's violent explosions and my mother's pleading voice. I hardly remember the circumstances or the facts. I only remember the world narrowing to the four walls of my rose-colored room and the bewildering uncertainty as the earth shifted beneath my feet.

Awakened by the sounds of shouting, I shuffled sleepily to my parents' room in my flannel nightie to witness them spitting angry words at each other. I froze just inside the door, watched them lash out at each other with fists and palms, saw my father catch my mother's flailing arms and shove her away. She fell back against the full-length mirror on the wall with a thud. A crack. Shocked silence. That's when they noticed me, kneeling on the floor, hands clasped together as if in prayer, tearfully begging them to stop.

He was gone the next morning.

The rest of us went on with our lives as if nothing had changed, except I got to take baths in my mother's bathroom. Before, when I'd had to use the hall bath, my brothers Richard and Mike liked to bang open the door and laugh at my naked, little girl body. (We weren't allowed to lock the bathroom door, in case we slipped and fell.) I complained, and

Mom said I could share the master bathroom with her. It would be "the girls' bathroom."

It was as though I had tossed a dime into the impossible glass bowl at the school fair and won the giant, pink Teddy bear. "Ha!" was all I said to Richard and Mike.

Now, as I prepared to bathe without fear of leering boys, I hummed a little tune, harmonizing with the low notes the rushing water made as it vibrated the tub and reverberated into the room. Standing before the sink mirror, I modeled, pulling my hair up and puckering my lips seductively. Not quite right. I reached into the cabinet for one of my mother's lipsticks, smeared the ruby color on my lips and cheeks, and repeated the pose, turning this way and that, one hand holding my hair up, the other perched on my hip, as I batted my eyes at my reflection. Glamorous. Silly. Giggling, I gave up on the pose and dropped my arms.

I put my shampoo bottle on the edge of the tub where I'd be able to reach it, then retrieved my mother's silver, double-edged razor from the medicine cabinet. A couple weeks before, she'd taught me how to shave my legs. Eight was a little young, she'd said, but I had a lot of dark hair on my legs and would I like to learn? Oh, yes! I'd said, imagining myself grown up and pretty, like my mother.

Freeing a new blade from its sleeve, I twisted the stem of the razor to open the two little barn doors on top, and holding the blade carefully as my mother had shown me, dropped it into its slot. Then I twisted the razor shut, giving the stem an extra turn to make sure it was tight, and laid it next to the shampoo. I tossed my clothes into the opposite corner and stepped into the steaming water—hot enough to make my skin flush a bright, joyful pink—and shut off the faucet. As the water covered me, the heat spread over my body and radiated into my bones.

My mother's bathroom had a single, porcelain sink, a metal-framed medicine cabinet, a bathtub, and a toilet—not luxurious by today's standards, but in that moment a galaxy of space all my own. My brothers would never bother me here, buffered as I was by the sanctity and expanse of my mother's bedroom.

Opposite the tub, above my pile of clothing, twilight filtered through the high, frosted window. Sheer, frilly-edged curtains softened the window's edges. My eyes followed their gentle curves, round and down and up again. Wallpaper patterned with tiny pink roses decorated two walls, contrasting with the plain, semi-gloss white on the other two. There were no pictures, but the flowered wallpaper made the room feminine, as though it had always belonged to just my mother and me.

I shampooed my hair and rinsed it by sinking all the way under water and swishing my head back and forth for as long as I could hold my breath, my short hair drifting like wet silk around my face. I soaped my body with a bar of Ivory, watching the soap swirling upward to create a milky skin on the water's surface.

I propped my left leg on the porcelain rim and lathered it until I could barely see my skin beneath the white foam. Concentrating hard on holding the razor straight and at just the right angle to avoid nicking myself, I drew it from ankle to knee, especially cautious over the bony parts—ankle, shin, and kneecap. Scraping off the little stubbles that grew back after the last shave still felt funny to me. I remembered that shaving-cream commercial on TV—what brand was that?—where the stubbles leapt out of the way when they saw the razor coming, and I wished Mom would let me try it. But she said that commercials were all lies and soap works just as well, maybe better. Someday I would have to shave under my arms too. I raised my right arm over my head, trying to see my armpit. I didn't know how I would ever do *that*. Shaving legs was hard enough.

I was still working on my left leg when my mother, wearing light-colored capris and a cotton blouse, entered the bathroom. She perched at the edge of my peripheral vision, on the closed lid of the toilet. Her blue eyes, bright and calculating, watched me.

"Look, Mom. I'm not cutting myself," I said proudly, without looking up.

"That's good," she said.

"Mom," I said, "why do I have such dark hair on my legs and arms? Mike and Richard have blond hair on theirs. And how come boys don't have to shave their legs?"

She paused. Then, as if she were revealing a fascinating tidbit of information to her students, she said, "Do you know that you really have two daddies?"

"Huh?" I looked up, razor paused midair. What did that have to do with leg hair?

She seemed amused by my confusion. "John Carr isn't your real daddy."

I stared at her, uncomprehending, trying to read her face, but it was impassive, as though she had said something inconsequential like, "nice day today." My mother's face was never without expression, unless she was trying to hide her feelings, so I knew whatever she was saying had to be important. How could Dad not be my daddy?

"Your daddy's name was John too," she said, "like John Carr, the daddy you know. They both call themselves 'Jack.'" She laughed a little. "But I called your daddy 'John,' to tell him apart from Jack."

John and Jack and Jack and John.

"About a year and a half before you were born, when I was thirty, I worked as a deputy sheriff in Alameda," she said. "That's where we met." Her eyes took on a faraway, dreamy look. "We were both new hires. On the first day of training, he was giving me change for a Coke, and when he put the quarter in my hand, a spark flew between us. That's how I knew." She glanced at me sideways, to see how I was taking her words. By now, I'd forgotten about shaving my legs.

"We began seeing each other after that," she said, and smiled with the memory. "He was a real take-charge kind of man." She sighed and fell silent, staring at the white wall for so long that I looked at the wall too. But there was nothing. I looked back at my mother and waited, afraid to break the spell of this moment, afraid that she would change her mind and I would never know what she meant by saying I had two daddies.

"He kept an apartment for us in Oakland. And he was an artist. You know the painting on my bedroom wall, the one overlooking the backyard with the woman hanging laundry?" I nodded. "He painted that. It was the view from our apartment."

She rushed on. "He drank a lot, though. Probably became an alcoholic and doesn't have his teeth any more, or went bald." She shrugged. "But he was a handsome man then. I've never really stopped loving him. Though I stayed married to Jack and would never have left him, I was always faithful to John in my heart."

She focused on me. "That's why you have dark hair and eyes, and your brothers have blond hair and blue eyes, and why you're the only girl. You're a love child."

"What's a 'love child'?"

"A love child comes from love between a man and a woman who are not married," she said. "I loved John and wanted to have his baby—I wanted and planned you—even though I was already married to Jack and had his boys."

The idea clicked into place like a puzzle piece. But this piece was the wrong color: it didn't match my picture, the one with Mom and Dad and my brothers and me. It matched another picture—my mother and a man with dark hair and dark eyes looking out the window of their secret apartment at a woman hanging clothes in her backyard, while my dad did what? Wondered where Mom was? Worried? Waited?

I imagined this man—my father?—putting his arm around my mother's shoulders. Kissing her. But she said he's probably bald and toothless. Why would she love someone like that? The bath water was cold. An image of my mother, pregnant with me, pushed itself into my imagination. I was not Jack Carr's; I was not my brothers' sister—or, no—I was their half-sister. Is that what it was called? I shuddered. I felt dizzy. I held still, but the world had gone sideways.

I grasped an idea. "Do I know him? Does he come to see me?"

"No. The last time I saw him, you were about five years old. Jack knew I went to see him. He was jealous, but he let me go. John was getting married. I think he has daughters now."

"You mean, I might have sisters?" I had always longed for a sister. I wondered if they looked like me, if I looked like *him*. I wished this man who was my real father, whatever that meant, would have loved me enough to stick around, that he would have waited for me.

But he didn't.

My real father had gone, just like Daddy. My stomach twisted into a cramp.

"Yes, half-sisters, I suppose. You might, someday, want to find him." Then she smiled, her manner light and cheerful in the way of adults when they think children don't understand the implications of something, when they think that smiles and happy voices will make everything all right.

"Time to get out now and get ready for bed." Then, she stood up and left the bathroom.

I sat upright in the tepid bathwater, gazing at the soap scum forming on the edges, vaguely registering the goose bumps that had risen on my arms and torso. She hadn't said so, but I knew this was a secret. I couldn't tell anyone. But how would I ever look at my brothers the same way? My mother? My dad!

Why had she told me?

I understood my parents were divorced, and my father had moved. I had lost the wholeness of my family, but at least I thought my dad was still my dad. Now, I had lost him in a new way, deeper, and more permanent.

My mother told me I had two daddies, but it seemed as though I had none. I might see Dad once in a while, but it wouldn't be the same. Did he love me? I had been unique because I was a girl, set apart from my brothers, even having my own room. But Dad hadn't taken me hunting like my brothers, and I couldn't remember ever sitting on his lap or being held by him. I know he loves me! I thought fiercely, holding onto the thought as if it would anchor me to my life. But I no longer felt sure of my place. I was a brunette, hazel-eyed girl, in a family of blond, blue-eyed boys. My difference had made me feel special and privileged; now I simply felt wrong.

I pulled the plug and watched the soapy water whirlpool downward and into the drain. I watched until gravity sucked the tub empty, leaving nothing but a ring of grime. Then I dried off, put on my favorite, cotton, baby doll pajamas, and went to bed.

JACKIE

I had always believed in Free Will, in my power to create my own destiny, that I create opportunities and build my future by making the right decisions. I always got what I wanted because I had the ability and the drive to accomplish my goals. But not when it came to love. In that one corner of my mind, I couldn't seem to control my thoughts, my actions, my self.

Ever since I was little, when the boys fought over me I liked it; flirting was fun, and nothing made me feel more attractive than attention from men. When I was in kindergarten, the neighbor boy and I shyly held hands. In first grade my "boyfriend" carried my books to class. And in second grade, I dropped my handkerchief for a boy to pick up, blushing when we touched. I had my first real date at nine. It was a Saturday matinee, and on the way home, my date bought a little green, glass elephant and gave it to me as a token of his love. That was only the beginning. By the time I was fourteen, boys were vying for my attention, trying to outdo one another with gifts of flowers and candy, and writing love letters and poems.

I went out with lots of boys. In high school, I dated Howard, Banker, Kenny, Jimmy, Ivan, Don, and Jack (who cried every time I went out with someone else). On weekends I worked as an usherette. From work, I dated Bill, Warren, Bud, Donald, and Charles, occasionally giving them a goodnight kiss, nothing more. I was careful. I never dated a man older than myself, because I wanted to be the one in control.

It was always difficult dividing my time among the boys, though, and I hated to hurt anyone's feelings. Even then, I didn't see why anyone should own me. The culture in which I lived said that I was supposed to date one boy at a time. But if I liked more than one boy, why should I do what the world wanted?

Jack, whom I met when we were both fifteen and dated throughout high school, waited faithfully for me and filled my cedar chest with linens and household items. He was jealous. Sometimes he ranted and raved and cried about the others, but we had known each other for over four years and he had plenty of time to know who I was.

Then the Japs bombed Pearl Harbor. The world was at war, all the boys were enlisting, and Jack asked me to marry him. I said yes. Later, I was seized with doubt, called my sister, and said, "I love him but I'm just not sure ... what should I do?"

"Make a list of the pros and cons," she said. So I did.

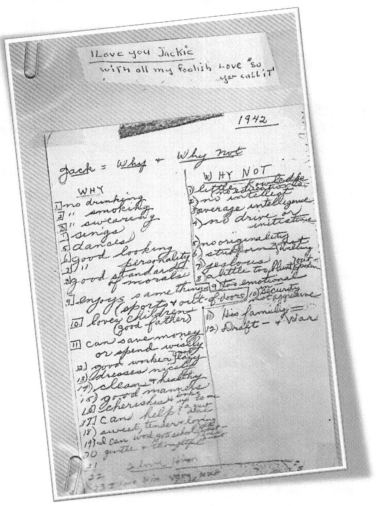

We were married on April 3, 1942.

When Terry was two weeks old, Jack was drafted into the Air Force. He was gone for three years. I worked hard to keep everything together—days teaching, and nights at the Army Hospital. Although I was often asked out, only once during those three years did I let go of my control, with a darling, good-looking soldier boy who also worked at the hospital. A sweet experience in the back of his car. But it scared me (in those days, no one would have understood), so I quit my job at the hospital and took another job as a household helper.

By the time Jack came home in 1945, I had earned my real estate license, bought and sold several homes, made money ironing and knitting, and did everything I could to add to Jack's income as an apprentice mechanic.

I loved Jack. I did. And we had a good marriage, as far as marriage goes. But still, I loved when men found me attractive and let me know it. Encounters with these men were exciting, dangerous, magnetic. I loved the fear. And I never felt guilty—only afraid of being caught.

The men in my life, 1942-1964:

1942:   *Married Jack*

1944:   *18-year-old serviceman, orderly at hospital*

1948:   *Whitey (met at dance); Jimmie (from college, both of us real estate agents)*

1950:   *Dick (spring and summer in Tahoe, summer of '50 in L.A.)*

1953:   *Bob, Paul, Ronnie (Berkeley police dept.); John (Alameda Deputy Sheriff - your father)*

1960-64: *Ed (math teacher); Bill S. (art teacher)*

1963-64: *Armand (from NY); Jim (spring in Acapulco); Royce (Thunderbird manager); Paul (dance instructor); Tom; Bob; Bill B (to 1969)*

1963 began badly. Jack and I had been working out a separation agreement; he'd even found a place to live, and we managed our schedules so that one of us would be with you kids each day. You and Mike didn't even know we were separated. You sensed it, of course, but you were too little to understand. Ricky started sucking his thumb again—I had to take him to the dentist and have one of those prong retainers installed—and hitting you and Mike when he thought I wasn't looking. John was furious with me, and with Jack, too. He wouldn't do anything we told him, and we were talking about sending him off to live with one of Jack's friends in Japan. I often thought that Terry was the only one who truly understood and accepted me for who I was. When I told him I'd decided to divorce his father, he surprised me by saying, "Mom, you'll never be happy with Dad. You need to be free to be you."

Anyway, in December, I was dating Ed, and Jack had started dating a younger woman named Barbara. Things weren't exactly easy, but they seemed to be coming along. Then, just after Christmas—a wonderful Christmas with kids and family and peaceful visits—Jack went to pieces and started hitting me in the car.

After that, fear was the key word in my relationship with Jack. I had to constantly placate him to keep his explosions to a minimum. He threatened me about money and you kids, one minute saying he was going to take you away from me, the next saying you were all mine and he'd refuse to spend time with you (and you know how that worked out). Or he threatened to make the affair with Ed public. I couldn't let that happen: I'd lose my job. It was all so damned depressing.

Even Ed and I were battling over stupid, little things. It seemed so easy to damage his ego, as if for me to be independent was the same as not being able to receive his love. We saw each other as often as possible. But I was afraid of not having any time for myself, and of trying to be all things to all people.

I didn't need anyone—that's what I thought. Maybe it was more a wish, than anything. I wanted to be free and didn't understand jealousy. I told Ed we were fighting too much, and I didn't want to see him anymore. Then, my first night alone, I got depressed and called him and he came over.

Sometimes, even though he was dating Barbara, Jack would come home and we'd spend such lovely, healing time together. He'd help around the house and spend time with you kids. When things were good between us, they were very good. On Valentine's Day, I had a drink after work with Ed, then dinner with Jack. He brought a box of candy, one for you, too, though you wouldn't remember it. He spent the night and we had a pleasant next day together, though we signed the papers to divide the property, which felt sad to me. I began to rethink the divorce and wondered if we could make it work after all—if only he could give me my freedom.

One night in late February, Ed and I and you three little ones were eating dinner together—a big spaghetti feed—when Jack walked in. When I saw him there, his face contorted and ugly, I froze.

Ed stood up. "I'll leave," he said.

I said, "I'm going too."

Jack turned and stomped upstairs to the bedroom. Ed and I left by the back door. Later, I phoned home to see what was going on.

Richard answered the phone. "Dad took his gun and shells."

I didn't know what to do. Ed and I went to see "Silence," a depressing movie, which depressed me further. I was afraid to go home, so I stayed with Ed and went home the next morning. Jack wasn't there. I stayed home all day, keeping busy with housework and worrying about him. Why did he take his gun? What had he done? I called Terry and asked him to find out what was going on.

When Terry called back, he said, "Dad took the gun to use on himself. He called his friend Curly, who came over, talked Dad out of it, and took the gun."

I never really thought Jack would do anything.

Why all the jealousy? I wanted to be able to love whomever I wanted whenever I wanted. And I wanted to be able to be honest about it. Instead, I had to juggle them, like so many balls: Jack, Ed, and then Bill, one after the other. Were the benefits of being loved worth feeling trapped and threatened? Who's to say? Were I to do it all over again, I wouldn't do anything differently.

I have tucked myself into a cushioned corner of the living room couch to read my mother's 1963 diary, hoping to find something of myself in its pages.

The word *FEAR* scrawled diagonally across the first page immediately confronts me. On the reverse side, she'd written, "that's the key word in my relationship with Jack at this time."

As I scan forward, I read about him hitting her, threatening her financially and physically. I'm only a few pages in, and I'm frozen in my chair, shocked by the violence of their fighting. I remember only the yelling. And that one time, that last fight, the hitting and shoving. I don't remember the other times, though my mother records some of it as having happened in front of us kids. Could I have blocked all this out of my mind? Is this why my memories of that time are so murky, as though I'm peering through scummy pond water?

Later that January, Mom wrote, "I arranged for a weekend in the snow for the entire family, but canceled it because I'm afraid to be off in the mountains with him. I feel so depressed and upset. ... I try to talk to Terry, but he's never available for anything but help for himself." I reflect on this last statement. I knew Mom habitually confided in Terry and asked for his advice, but it must have been hard on him. In January of 1963, he was nineteen. How could my mother expect him to be her counselor, to expose him so intimately to all that was going on between his mother and father?

Reading on, I learn that my mother awoke early every day, fed us breakfast, and sent us to school before going to work at Hillsdale High School; evenings she taught group therapy sessions, attended classes, and went out afterwards for drinks and dancing, returning home and climbing into bed only a few hours before starting all over again. Just reading about it exhausts me.

I learn that my mother and father were already divorced when my mother wrote *FEAR* onto the first page of her diary; although he had an apartment elsewhere, he still lived part-time at the house. I always thought the divorce happened later. As a child, I had sensed that things between my parents were strained and complicated, and I knew my mother was changing, but I hadn't known what was really going on.

According to her diary, my mother fought with Jack because she wanted freedom to be with Ed. She fought with Ed because she wanted freedom to be with Jack—and Bill, another teacher at the high school where she and Ed taught. (Ed and Bill were married men.) She broke up and made up with each in turn. When they broke up, there was hitting and being "knocked around," and when they made up, there was "sweet, loving time together." In the midst of all this fighting and loving, she was out meeting new men, flirting, and soaking up their desire for her.

Every night there was a different guy: Glen, Jimmie, Jacque, Bill, Ed, Luis, Pablo ... the names seem endless. Reading her diary is like watching a deranged fisherman reeling in fish, one after another, only to throw them back in the water. And the fish, disoriented and hungry, go for the bait again, over and over in an endless, destructive cycle.

She wrote about going with Ed to visit her Aunt Dottie and there meeting Armand, "a negro singer from N.Y." She and Armand "played kneesees" under the table while she sat next to Ed. She arranged to meet Armand for a date the following night. According to my mother's diary, that was a typical day.

A week in my mother's life:

Fri: *Fed the kids, went on school field trip to San Francisco with Art Dept. Spent night afterwards, with Bill (art teacher). Wonderful.*

Sat: *Home by 10:00 am, then spent the afternoon with Ed. We had a lovely, sweet time. After dinner, Jack went out with the boys and*

I went to the Thunderbird for drinks with my friend, JoAnn. Met two cute salesmen. Afterwards, I went to Ed's and spent the night.

Sun: *Got home at 6:00 am to find Jack's truck out front and Jack in my bed. Furious, he shouted, "This is the last time you'll ever see me." After he left, I went to bed and slept most of the day. Glen, one of the salesmen I met the night before, phoned. Took me to the Shadows for dinner. Afterwards, we danced at the Thunderbird and then to the Villa. An interesting, perceptive young man.*

Mon: *Home by 1:00 am. Bill picked me up after work and we went to the beach in San Francisco, had hamburgers and milkshakes for dinner. I didn't go to my night class. Bill's quite an artist, and an amateur psychologist—I hope to learn about painting from him. Sensitive, quiet guy.*

Tues: *Home by 6:40 am, fed the kids, then off to work. Had a furious battle with Ed. I think he's really through this time. Jack phoned, said he'd take me to the Senior Ball on Saturday night. After he phoned, he came over and spent the night. Sometimes, we're so happy together.*

Wed: *After work, drove to Ed's to return the key to his apartment. Ended up staying until 2:00 am. He said, "Goodbye Jackie. You're taking my heart with you." A loving end to our relationship.*

Thurs: *An hour after school, Ed phoned. He said, "Get rid of the kids at the meeting tonight, because I'm coming over. I'll settle for one night a week." We fought. I thought he had meant it when he said it was over. He showed up at the end of the H.S. session. Glen phoned while he was there and Ed got jealous. We fought. He pulled my hair, pushed me, held me in a chair. I cried. Hated him! Afterwards, Glen picked me up and quieted me.*

In April, on what would have been their 20th anniversary, Jack beat her up after he came home to find her in bed with Ed. Even though they were divorced and even though he had known about Ed for a long time, he was unable to control his jealous rage. The next day, my eighth birthday, she wrote, "We put the house up for sale as a result of last night's fight. I'm hurting all over today. Bruised arms and legs, skinned elbows, cut mouth and lips." My dad apologized, but only four days later he hit her again.

Mom see-sawed between excitement and depression. At one point, when she had broken up with them all and had been alone for just one day, she wrote,

> I'm feeling lost. Ed's gone. Bill's gone. Jack's gone. Jim's far away, and nothing for the future anyway.... a whole day—waiting for a phone call—for anyone who might care for me. I've been writing through all of this terrible, deep depression. Everyone has failed me.

Within three days, she initiated contact with Jack and Ed, and began going out at night to meet other men again.

By October, Jack was staying away for longer periods, up to four or five days, but Ed and my mother continued to fight about her seeing other men. On the 17th, after a date dropped her at home at 2:00 a.m., "Ed broke into the house and beat me up real bad. I got away and hid in the bushes in the back of the yard." She waited until Ed left, then got my brother John to take her to her friend Joanne's house. The next day, she phoned Ed and asked him to take her to the hospital. She had black eyes, a bruised face, cut-up mouth, bruised tailbone and legs, and a broken hand.

She was back home and loaded up on Codeine for the pain when Jack came over and asked her to marry him again. "I love him, but I can't," she wrote. "Sweet and tender moment between us, but so sad." After Jack left, Ed called, and they talked, "trying to understand each other."

More than forty-five years later, I sit here on my comfortable couch trying to understand my mother, aghast at her frenetic infidelity and unable to comprehend why she would want these men. How could she put up with being beaten and then make excuses for their behavior? This is not the mother I knew. Not the strong woman who used men for her own purposes. Not the woman who was always on the cutting edge of progressive thinking. I have a vague recollection of her being bruised by a car accident. Was that just a cover-up?

I feel guilty because I can't help judging her, and I'm beginning to wonder if she was manic-depressive.

I don't know what I expected when I opened this diary, but certainly not this. I had thought—or hoped—that her diary would be something like mine, filled with hopes and dreams for her future, emotional responses and reactions to her day, including her relationships with her children—that what she recorded would be more like what I remember.

I shuffle through the pages, searching the diary for my name. But, for the most part, we children are only mentioned on birthdays, when we have doctor's appointments, dancing lessons, or are ill, our needs documented as additional details in a busy life. On Halloween that year, there is no mention of children at all. No costumes or trick-or-treating. She has gone out for the evening, dancing and drinking.

I can only wonder, *Where was I?*

Sabbatical

Plucked from my mother's treasure trove of boxes, four thick binders labeled "World Tour" have waited patiently on a bookshelf in my office. I've been afraid to open them—afraid my mother's versions of events will be too different from my own, or swallow my memories whole, altering them in some fundamental, irrevocable way. I want to hold onto my own versions of our trip around the world, seen and understood through my childish eyes. But that year-long journey with my mother is too important to skip over: it maps the point between child and pre-teen, between closeness and separation; it marks the expansion of my world view; and, I feel sure, marks my mother's transition from married to independent woman, and full-time mother to full-time seeker.

After Dad left for good, Mom decided to "run away from home," which meant taking a sabbatical from teaching, selling our house, disposing of all our possessions except for what we could carry, and embarking on a 365-day trip around the world with John, Mike, and me. John planned to travel with us only through the first month before going off on his own. Richard, at fourteen, didn't want to go and went to stay with our Aunt Bev. Mom, Mike, and I would round the earth in an easterly direction and visit sixty different countries during the year.

While we traveled, my mother wrote daily, and later meticulously transcribed her journals and notes into WordStar on her vintage IBM computer. Then she printed, three-hole-punched, and placed all 678 pages into these four binders.

Taking a deep breath for courage, I pull the first volume—a plain, black vinyl binder—off the shelf. The scotch tape holding the yellowed, typed label is brittle and peeling with age, so I apply fresh tape to re-secure it. Inside the front cover lies a receipt for $6,489.30 from Sally Morrison Travel—the cost for four, good-for-one-year, round-the-world airplane tickets, plus a brand new Volkswagen camper, reservations for one night at the New York Taft Hotel, and tickets to the 1965 World's Fair. So much for so little, I think, though I'm sure it seemed like a lot of money at the time. My mother had written, "I don't know enough geography to make plans. I don't know where we will go. I plan to get visas and permits as we travel. We will play it by ear."

The volume spans June 21 to August 19, during which time we traveled from San Francisco to New York, and then through Ireland, Scotland, England, the Netherlands, Belgium, Germany, Denmark, Sweden, Norway, Finland, and, my mother alone, to Russia. There is a picture of the three of us standing on the red brick steps of our house, suitcases in hand, and a letter—a preface, really—dated August 20, 1985.

In the last 20 years, I was too busy living life to write about our trip around the world, 1965 to 1966. But greater deterrents were that I couldn't find either a motivation or audience for taking the time to rehash the past. Another deterrent is the fear of disclosing one's imperfections. To be honest requires showing one's smallness of character.

I told myself that I must write about our trip around the world for my children and my grandchildren. I have enjoyed reviewing stories about Mike when he was eight years old, and Linda when she was ten. At times Mike was a source of humor to lighten up the drudgery of travel. At times Linda was a comfort and a sage. Yet, I suspect they will be busy living their lives rather than taking the time to wade through these many pages to find themselves.

Ultimately, it's only possible to write through one's own view of the world—feelings, biases, confusions. Such writing is too personal and egocentric for any audience other than the self. I am embarrassed about focusing on myself and worse, disappointed. At times I want to disown the main character in this story because she is not a "heroin." I find my foibles, weaknesses, and unheroic qualities unacceptable. Much of the writing shows my personal struggles with guilt, resentment, and anxiety. At times, I do not like the person I find here.

Yet, buried in the personal is an historical document of the world in 1965 to '66, which includes disputes between countries: the Berlin wall, (East and West Germany); Spain and Britain at Gibraltar; Turks versus Greeks; Israel versus the Arab; Karachi and India; Thailand and Cambodia; North and South Vietnam; North and South Korea.

Much of this document, like a diary, simply recounts daily events which are often boring. But life is often boring. It would be dishonest to simply write about the exciting parts. Because I wanted to write "the way it was," the story lacks the qualities of fiction. I wish my life were like fiction, but it is not. These pages, like life, are filled with dull days, exciting days, forgettable days and memorable days. ...

Life cannot be captured like a butterfly in a net nor can it be mounted in a frame and hung on the wall. It can only be lived. This year, 1965 to 1966, was one of my most memorable.

I am touched—and surprised—by my mother's self-awareness and honesty, and by how much I resonate to her prose. By the third page, it is as though I am viewing two movies in my mind: my mother's recounting of events, and my own memories of them, awakened and tagging along like puppies.

These journals, like her 1963 diary, rise and dip between excitement and fear, happiness and depression. Her writing, because she is writing for herself, is more raw and real than her letters. In the beginning of our trip, she was often afraid, especially at night.

> *What am I doing in Europe with my eight-year-old son and ten-year-old daughter? Satisfying my obsession with freedom by ending my twenty-two-year marriage? ... I have been feeling smug about how much more free I am than anyone I know, free to have extricated myself from a perfectly good marriage to a man I still love, who loves me, just to prove to myself that I am free. Free enough to have sold my home, furniture, all worldly possessions, everything that rooted us to permanence, to one spot on this Earth. I uprooted my children and took off, like an eagle with chicks on its back as if I had no human limitations. The image is ludicrous.*

Publicly, my mother had expressed only confidence in her sense of direction in life and dismissed any suggestion that her actions might have negative impacts. So this acknowledgment of doubt startles me, and I feel a surge of respect for the courage it took to go on such a journey with two small children.

For the first month, beginning in Scotland, traveling through the British Isles and north, we rented cars and stayed in youth hostels. Though we traveled together, Mom often left us with John for hours at a time while she explored on her own or went to pubs. While attending conferences or traveling by herself, she found places for Mike and me to stay. In Copenhagen, she sent us to a summer camp by the ocean while she attended a week-long workshop.

In London, she placed Mike and me in an English "nursery school," while she modeled for a pastel artist named Maurice Man in exchange for her choice of portraits. She modeled for ten days. I had forgotten all about Maurice Man, but images now flood my mind. I remember the nursery school as a large, three-story building surrounded by park-like grounds. I remember that the four of us stayed with Maurice and his wife Valerie the last three days we were in London. And I remember feeling privileged and grownup and beautiful as I sat before the artist with my mother one afternoon, both of us naked except for strategically wrapped sheets. Man broke his promise, however, and never sent the portraits Mom selected.

Fortunately, she took pictures of them. Now, gazing at the page on which she clumsily pasted the pictures, I think the two portraits that best capture my mother are one with three poses draped in white, and the one in which she is reading.

Curious, I perform an Internet search for Man and discover that he made portraits for a number of famous people, including Joan Collins, Julie Andrews, and Natalie Wood. He died in 1997. I wish Man had sent those portraits of my mother.

In Frankfurt, we picked up our Volkswagen van—"home" for Mom, Mike, and me for the following four months—while John left to travel on his own. After that, though we sometimes still slept at youth hostels or—on rare occasions—hotels, we mostly slept at campgrounds or by the side of the road.

And though Mom frequently left us with others, I have distinct memories of only three occasions: a family in Sweden while she traveled to Finland and Russia, a Spanish family in Barcelona while I attended the American School for three months, and an American family on a naval base near Tokyo, in Sagamihara, Japan while she traveled to Korea and Vietnam. (In each instance, she found a separate placement for Mike.)

I've often wondered how she found places for us to stay. It turns out to have been planning by opportunity. For example, while she made arrangements to travel behind the Iron Curtain to Russia, we stayed at a campground near Stockholm. There, I made friends with another girl my age—Helen, from Sweden. When Helen's family was leaving, my mother said, "I'm sorry you're leaving. I was hoping you'd stay long enough to get acquainted so that when I go to Russia, maybe Linda could visit you." Then,

> Helen hopped out of the camper, ran over to her father, brought him back, introduced him to me. He's a teacher, too. Within ten minutes, Linda was packed and gone. ... After they were gone, I had second thoughts. ... I trust my intuition, but that doesn't stop my head from doing 'tricks,' filling with doubts. I wondered what they thought of American mothers who let their ten-year-old daughters go with strangers.

As a parent and grandparent now, I can't imagine it. But it turned out I was safe with Helen's family. Mike went to a summer camp in Finland, where he was the only child, gladly soaking up the extra adult attention.

After I went away with Helen, and before Mike went to Finland, my mother left him alone in the van at night while she went dancing. She'd tell him to lock the car doors and not to open them to anyone. Then she'd wait until he fell asleep and go into a hotel restaurant. One night, she met a Swedish drum player. After his set was done at 1:00 a.m., they went to the Flamingo, a Swedish nightclub, driving "for what seemed a long time." She returned to the van at 6:00 a.m. Mom recorded many nights like this.

"I am bothered by my age," she wrote. "Most men … think I'm close to thirty when in fact I'm forty-two. I don't feel flattered but anxious because I believe they would not be as interested in me if they knew my age."

Her drummer had been married to a Japanese prostitute and, after their second night together said to my mother, "Are you sure you're not a prostitute?" She took this as a compliment.

There are other things my mother, driven by a desire for adventure, did that I judge as reckless. Once, after meeting a young man at a restaurant in Spain, my mother impulsively agreed to tour Spain, Gibraltar, Tangiers, and Lisbon with him, essentially spending two weeks cooped up in her little Volkswagen van with a stranger.

She slept, wakeful and tense by his side for three nights, waiting for him to make a move. When he finally did roll over in the night and slip his hands under her clothes, she let him touch her "without tenderness or affection," her mind blank, her body accepting.

Afterward, she wrote,

> For the first time in my life, sex with a man was not buried in sweet words of love. I did not believe Jerry was capable of tenderness, romance, or even affection. I did not believe Jerry capable of feeling … Strangely, I did not have an emotional response either.

I wonder why, when Jerry proved to be racist, prone to violent rages, and a drinker, my mother continued to travel with him. Though I understand, after reading her travelogues, that she set out to explore her inner terrain as much as the outer world, her behavior alarms me, even after all this time and when there is no chance of harm. Yet, when I was forty-two, the same age my mother was then, I also explored sex without love. I also tried out the "one night stand." I ultimately decided that sex without affection is empty and dull, while she craved the excitement and danger of it. Does that make me more moral?

The American School in Barcelona made arrangements for Mike and me to board with Spanish families during fall semester. Before the semester began, we were supposed to meet Michael's family in La Costa Brava, so my mother decided to make an adventure of it by driving north across Spain into the Pyrenees Mountains to visit the small country of Andorra. We would then cross into France and drive back down the eastern edge of Spain to La Costa Brava.

As our van climbed the narrow mountain road into Andorra, we passed isolated farmhouses, quaint villages, and lush green valleys. Everything sparkled in the clear, sunlit air. We stopped for a lunch of French bread and cheese on a dam overlooking a reservoir. For dessert, all three of us stole red apples from a nearby apple orchard, giggling wildly as we ran away, pockets bulging.

Reaching the picturesque village of Andorra la Vella mid afternoon, we walked around town, bought a patch for Michael's jacket, a silver charm for my bracelet, and some postcards—the only souvenirs we were allowed. Soon, though, the weather turned cold and started to rain. We were freezing, dressed as we were for the warmth of lower altitudes, so Mom decided it was time to leave.

The road climbed, then narrowed as it twisted and turned between towering cliffs and sheer drops unprotected by guardrails. As afternoon waned to twilight, snow began to fall and thick fog reduced our visibility even more. Mike fell asleep in the back of the van, but I clutched the door handle, tense in the passenger seat. Mom drove as quickly as she dared to get us down the dangerous mountain before nightfall, but as we passed through the last inhabited village, the light winked and disappeared.

Mom concentrated on the road revealed by the ghostly glare of our headlamps. I concentrated on my mother, tried not to think about the edge of the road so close to my door, and willed her to make us safe. Approaching a hairpin curve, I felt the wheels slide sideways. As my side of the van drifted in slow motion toward the edge, which gave way to a yawning black precipice, I gripped the door handle and closed my eyes.

I thought we flew off the road.

When the car spun and struck something with a *bang!* turning and banging again and again and again, I pictured us falling to our deaths, hitting jutting ledges of rock on our way down. I heard high-pitched screaming and wondered with strange detachment who was screaming before realizing it was me. I clamped my mouth shut. The screaming stopped. Unexpectedly, we came to a halt, rocking and listing to one side. I opened my eyes, surprised to find myself alive and still on the road. The left side of the van had hit the mountain with such force we had spun around, hit the other side of the van, and spun again before coming to rest, facing the same direction we'd been traveling.

Mike, who had fallen to the floor in the back, sat up and asked, "What was that?"

No one replied.

Mom sat pale and stunned in her seat, which had been torn out of its sockets and sat crookedly a few inches from the steering wheel. If someone came around the corner, we were in a bad spot. She turned the key in the ignition and the car started, but when she turned the steering wheel nothing happened. The van limped a few feet to the gravel at the cliff edge of the road. My mother braked, put the car in park, and turned on the emergency flashers. We unlatched our seat belts and tried to get out, but neither of the front doors would budge. So Mom crawled into the back, slid open the side door, and climbed outside to investigate. I crawled out after her. The front bumper was bent upward in a smiling curve over the doors, locking us in. Both front wheels sagged under the van. It was obvious even to me that the van would be going nowhere that night.

When lights alerted us that a car was coming up the road, we tried to flag it down, waving and shouting, but it passed without slowing. Several cars passed. Even with our jackets, which we'd retrieved from our suitcases, we were numb with cold. Just when we were resigned to sleeping in the van, a car stopped. The driver, a man, gave us a lift down the mountain to the village of Puigcerda, to a small hotel, and made sure we had a room before he left us.

Once in our room, the three of us, shivering and exhausted, crawled into a large double bed and fell asleep.

It took two days for the garage to cobble together the van so my mother could drive *muy despacio*, very slowly, retracing our path up over the mountain, past the scene of our accident, and then five hours to La Costa Brava, where we met and left Mike with his Spanish family.

The next morning, in the predawn hours, Mom woke and began driving our crippled van toward Barcelona, where she hoped we would find a repair garage. But she kept getting lost in the dark, unable to find the main highway. The roads were full of ruts and, terrified the car would fall apart stranding us in the middle of nowhere, she started to cry. She cried so hard, she couldn't see and had to stop the car. Together, we sat, as the sun emerged, a flaming red ball over the Mediterranean sea. Small fishing boats bobbed gently in the water.

My mother sobbed and sobbed, and I didn't know what to do. Then I remembered how much she loved sunrises and sunsets. I took her hand and said, "Mommy, look at the sun coming up over there." She looked up and in a moment was quiet, shuddering but no longer sobbing. "There," I said, "Feel better now?"

She nodded and squeezed my hand. After the sun was high over the water, she started the van and drove to Barcelona.

JACKIE

In all those different countries, many people were kind to us, like the Swedish family that took you in and the man who stopped in the Pyrenees Mountains. Though at first I'd been afraid to travel alone, I began to realize that not many people have the opportunity to learn what I learned during our travels: 1) to be a little bit crazy (a la Zorba the Greek); 2) to have a basic faith and trust in human beings; and 3) to have the "gall" to ask for help. Priceless lessons that I hoped you learned, as well.

In Barcelona, you did well in school. The lady you lived with wanted to keep you forever, because you were so good and clean and well-behaved. A happy, affectionate ten-year-old girl, you would throw your arms around my neck and kiss me. I never worried about you, though we went through a period of uncertainty—each time we said goodbye, not knowing what to expect, each of us trying to perceive the feelings of the other. A watchful, waiting, wordless time that tested our needs for dependence and independence.

When you kids went to stay with your families, the prospect of nights alone in the camper, where I would not speak to anyone, frightened me. Underneath it all, I was afraid of getting older. I wished I were a little girl and someone would take care of me and buy the food and make the decisions and do the driving.

But I never was a child. My father couldn't take care of me. I didn't marry a man who could take care of me. I wouldn't have settled for Aga Khan himself, because it would have cost me my freedom. I knew I would just have to learn to tolerate my own imperfections, because I was really the only one I could depend upon.

One of the reasons I'd decided to take that trip around the world was a desire to write. It was in my consciousness a dozen times every day, the words in my head, coming out of my mouth, and spilling from my fingers onto paper. But I had no faith that I had the ability to write, and I didn't know where or how to begin. At night, I'd fret: What kind of writer did I want to be? Would I have to give up living? I loved teaching. I loved the excitement of moving all over the world. When would I find time to write? Hard work and discipline would not be enough. I was not creative or talented enough.

Another fear had to do with my defective memory, fear of the darkness in the cave where my own experiences were buried. I owned very little of my life. My life happened to me and the events recorded on film had run off the reel. I couldn't rerun the film because it melted in the heat and speed of living.

I was afraid I couldn't find the key that would unlock the mystery of myself. Or worse, perhaps there was nothing there—just a hollow shell that spent a life being busy, looking busy, acting busy: growing up, school, marriage, a war, kids, lovers, education, progression. I lacked the wisdom to understand who I was or what I wanted.

After a few nights camping alone, I began to lose some of my fear, even enjoyed being alone because it was a choice. I wondered, could I learn to be alone and enjoy doing nothing? Having no goals? Without "accomplishing" something? Yes, I thought I could. A whole life could be spent having no goals, doing nothing, accomplishing nothing.

It was all so new to me, after years of family life—actually a whole life with family—that feeling of wanting to be alone. At night, I lay awake talking to my phantom students. I would be a really good teacher, better than ever when I got back home. I loved the excitement of energizing other people, but at that time in my life—my time alone in that little camper—I felt content and at peace in my aloneness.

A Man's World

Clouds are gathering outside as I slide my mother's third travel journal from the bookshelf and settle into my reading chair. I open the volume—a recycled, textured brown leather binder embossed with the title of a real estate firm—and caress the thin paper with my fingertips. Postcards, brochures, tickets, and photos cover the backs of the pages. A nagging sense of restless discomfort blossoms in my awareness, forcing me to acknowledge heightened feelings of ambivalence toward my mother. I have begun to see her in a different light: confused and trying desperately to figure out who she was and to define her place in the world, while battling cultural conditioning and restraints. Because I have endured my own version of that search and battle, including a divorce after eighteen years of marriage, I feel the old Tar of anger and resentment softening, stretching, and thinning as something like sympathy displaces it. A change, I realize with dismay, that I'm resisting.

I have spent a lifetime defining myself in opposition to my mother. I would like to think I never put my children at risk the way she did, but my mind drifts backward in time to after my divorce: the times I left my children with babysitters who were, I know now, too young; the times I recklessly brought the men I was dating into my children's lives; the times I sent my children to camp so I could experience the peace of solitude.

I, like my mother, have been a risk-taker, though not in the same way or to the same degree. She understood better than I that risk and adventure are coupled; everything, including getting out of bed in the morning, entails some degree of risk. I'm reminded of Helen Keller's famous quote: "Life is either a daring adventure or nothing. Security does not exist in nature, nor do the children of men as a whole experience it. Avoiding danger is no safer in the long run than exposure." Without my mother's willingness to gamble on the good nature of others, what life experiences might I have missed?

Those gambles increased in number and intensity after John and the Volkswagen camper departed from Genoa on a freight ship bound for the United States. Mom, Mike, and I left Spain and continued our tour by plane and bus across Italy, Vienna, Yugoslavia, Romania, Greece, Turkey, and the Middle East.

The world of 1965 belonged to men. Everywhere we went my mother was the only woman traveling alone with children and without the protection of a man. I knew we stood out for this reason, but I was too young to understand my mother's fears, how difficult it was to navigate the language barrier in each new country, or how concerned about money she was.

In spite of her fears, she rarely planned ahead, finding hotels, meals, and helpful people along the way. She encouraged us to be flexible, take delays and inconveniences in stride, and see each change of plan as a new opportunity for adventure. Mike and I learned to make friends rapidly, but without attachment, because we'd soon be saying goodbye. In each new place, my mother would find someone to guide us for cheap or free, in exchange for English language practice. And our guides would introduce us to family or friends with whom we'd share meals, and who sometimes generously invited us to stay in their homes.

And everywhere we went, men wanted to claim my mother—some for companionship, some for sex, some for control, and some for all three. She liked it when men desired her, whether she desired them or not, and took lovers whenever it suited her. The more forceful a man was, the more passive she became. And because most men wouldn't threaten her or force their affections on a woman in the presence of children, Mom kept us by her side for protection. I liked that role and suspect that Mike did too. We knew our mother was different from other mothers; men wanted her, and we were her best insurance of safety.

But in Greece and Turkey, I'd clutch her hand when we walked down the streets, because men would grope me as they passed, not even caring that I was with my mother. When I told Mom, she laughed lightly and said to ignore them, but I noticed afterward that she pulled me closer to her when men walked by.

In Istanbul, just after Christmas, we met a dark-skinned harp player named Celso who also happened to be staying at our hotel. Tight, black curls framed his high cheekbones and deep brown eyes, and his white teeth flashed when he smiled. The fingers of his hands were delicate and tapered, with manicured nails kept long for plucking the harp strings. I went with my mother to Klub-X, where his band played, and watched through a haze of curling cigarette smoke as his slim fingers moved over the strings. He was so beautiful and young and naive that even I fell a little in love with him, jealous whenever he paid more attention to my mother than to me. Mom decided to stay a few extra days in Istanbul just to be near Celso, who wrote poetry and songs for us, and showed me how to play flamenco guitar.

On New Year's Eve, planning to meet Celso afterward at Klub-X, we went to the Hilton to splurge on ice cream. There, my mother met an

American man who said he was a photographer for *Playboy*. Dave was one of those muscled, handsome, take-charge men who made a habit of refusing to take no for an answer. Sensing that he would ruin everything with Celso, I disliked him immediately.

Later, when my mother told him we were leaving to meet friends at Klub-X, he insisted on taking us there.

In the car, my mother told him, "We're leaving Istanbul in the morning."

"Nonsense," he said. "Cancel your flight. You and the kids can come back to the Hilton with me, and tomorrow I'll show you *my* Istanbul."

"I've already changed our flight once," she said. "I can't do it again."

I don't remember what happened when we arrived at the club, only that before the night was over, Dave, Celso, two members of his band, my mother, Mike, and I were all crowded into our little hotel room arguing over whether my mother should go to the Hilton with Dave or stay with Celso. The two men circled each other like roosters ready to battle over possession of the hen.

But Celso was sweet and gentle, and no match for the macho Dave. He said to my mother, "I love you. If you want to go, it's all right."

Mike told Mom she should go with Dave.

I cried and yelled at Dave to go away and leave us alone.

The band members sat in the doorway smoking cigarettes.

No one seemed to care what my mother wanted. She even tried to discourage both twenty-nine-year-old men by telling them her age (a fact she rarely revealed), but that only fueled their ardent declarations.

In the end, Mom sent Dave away. Feeling wounded, Celso retreated to his room.

The next day, Celso took us to lunch. My mother kissed him one last time. Then we took a taxi to the airport. As we waited in the boarding area, three uniformed men strode purposefully across the room toward us. The man in front was Dave.

We stared open-mouthed while Dave ordered the baggage clerk to give him our bags—the clerk obeyed without question—and then hustled us with all our luggage out of the airport and into a waiting car. The two men we didn't know got into the front while Dave got into the back with us. They drove us to the Hilton, where Dave had reserved a two-room suite. On the way there, he explained that he was actually a captain in the U.S. Army and on his first leave in five months.

"When I see something I want, I take it," he said.

"How do you decide what you want?" my mother asked. But I could see that she wasn't really listening to his answer—something about "class" and "character"—she just seemed dazed, paralyzed by the force of this man.

Mike was happy about not having to get on another airplane, but I didn't like Dave. Our presence had been no protection against him, which made me feel helpless and worried. At the same time, the drama exhilarated me.

It turned out that Dave had to return to base the following day. When I realized nothing bad was going to happen, I let down my guard and saw the whole thing as another adventure. Mike and I had a grand time running through the Hilton's hallways, riding on the elevators, and throwing paper airplanes from our top floor balcony. That night, we slept in the bedroom next to the room Dave and our mother shared.

In the morning, Dave took us out to breakfast and said goodbye. He told my mother he'd paid for everything, but she later discovered he'd lied. So she paid the Hilton and moved us to a smaller hotel across the street.

On a bus from Jerusalem to Cairo, we met Hosni, a light-skinned Egyptian who chatted with my mother for most of the ride. Before we arrived, he offered to be our guide in Cairo in exchange for the opportunity to practice English.

Cairo bustled with people and animals, the air filled with the cacophony of cars and buses honking, people shouting, and music blaring. Hosni took us to Egyptian bazaars, their tiny shops packed with bright-colored wares and teeming with people. We went to the Citadel, and visited mosques and palaces. We rode a boat across the Nile River and went out into the desert where we climbed the claustrophobically small passageway into the burial room of the Great Pyramid. We rode bad-tempered camels and tasted a drink made from crushed sugar cane (horrible). And we ate spiced dishes, made of beans and vegetables and roasted lamb and onions, that set our tongues on fire so that Mike and I waved our hands frantically in front of our mouths, causing our servers to roar with laughter.

Men and boys dangled from the outside of the buses and trolleys, which listed crazily to one side or the other and merely slowed to allow people to jump on or off at the "stops." As we watched, a woman attempted to get onto one bus with her toddler. The toddler stepped off as the bus driver closed the door and started down the road, the woman screaming for her child, arms stretched out the window. No one, except us, seemed to take any notice or express concern for her, and the driver didn't halt the bus until the next scheduled stop, blocks away. The mother jumped off, still screaming, and ran all the way back to where her abandoned child now played in the dust by the side of the road.

"Human life has no value to these people," my mother told us. "Their donkeys are worth more to them than their children."

I looked around and decided she must be right—the animals *were* being taken care of, while women and children were not—and thought how lucky I was not to have been born in Cairo.

That evening, Hosni invited us to a "real Egyptian nightclub." Mike said he didn't want to go, so Mom left him in the care of a fellow tourist. We climbed into a taxi with Hosni, my mother and I in the back holding hands while Hosni sat in front chatting with the taxi driver, and sped away from the night noise of the city and out into the silent desert. At first, Mom tried to keep up a conversation with Hosni, but finding it difficult to talk over the clatter of the car, she fell silent and looked out the window.

We drove for what felt like hours, deeper and deeper into the desert. We didn't even seem to be on a road, and I couldn't understand how the taxi driver knew where to go. My mother's hand tightened over mine until I pulled away, complaining. I wondered why she didn't seem excited. I loved music and dancing and the feeling of being included in the adult world she inhabited. Since leaving the United States, I'd been to many nightclubs in Europe, but this would be my first in the Middle East, and I was filled with anticipation.

But the beauty outside my window soon made me forget all about the nightclub. Silhouetted by a brilliant full moon, the three pyramids loomed before us, black and solid and imposing. Above their sharp peaks, the stars sparkled. At their feet, ethereal colors undulated over the surface of the sand in translucent and mystical rainbow waves. I held my breath, afraid to blink in case the vision disappeared.

Then we came over a rise, and a large tent—larger than a circus big top—emerged before us. The taxi parked near the entrance, and Hosni escorted us inside where a wide band of tables circled a large performance ring. He found a table for us close to the ring, where African dancers in elaborate, colorful costumes were at that moment performing. Then two exotic girls danced while balancing tall candelabras on their heads and tables on their chins. A little boy, about six, danced and performed acrobatics with a group of robed men whose long hair reached halfway down their backs. Belly dancers stepped into the ring, shimmying and gyrating to the rhythms of drums, while we ate hot-spiced Oman salad and roasted lamb.

The audience, nearly all men, was lively—whistling and shouting and smoking. We were the only white people in the tent, which made us objects of interest. After the belly dancers were done, everyone got up and danced. I did too. A photographer came over and took my picture with Hosni and the little acrobat.

Filled with exuberant exhaustion, my mother and I arrived back at the hotel and collapsed into our beds just before dawn.

JACKIE

In that Istanbul hotel showdown, everyone lost. Even though I sent Dave away, Celso was hurt. I felt I had rejected Dave as a human being. At the time, I felt embarrassed and ashamed—evil. I hated it all and, at the same time, it was unbelievably, marvelously crazy to have met two men who both wanted me at the same time. It was new and unbelievable every time it happened, even in small ways.

Like the flight from Vienna to Bucharest, when I met the British Embassy official. My "Viennese Friend"—the man who had shown us around Vienna and flirted with me—was also on the flight. When we arrived at the Bucharest airport, I found myself between these men. Both spoke Romanian.

"Torn between two men," I felt confused. But, my confusion turned into resentment as I attempted to get through customs and immigration, and past visa officials. Honestly, I could have done better by myself because officials usually just let me through with my children. With both men interpreting for us, it took longer.

But through all that we experienced, we learned to bend with the wind. The waiting, delays and inconveniences became easier all the time as we changed our attitude to seeing the adventure.

I always trusted my gut when it came to people, and I was rarely wrong. But in Cairo, as we drove miles away from civilization, I began to have wild visions of my little girl and "white slavery," whatever that was. And I was greatly relieved when we finally arrived at the nightclub, that colorful tent way out in the desert. We had a wonderful experience we would never have had if I hadn't trusted people along the way.

My biggest worries were actually about what was happening back home. I hadn't heard whether John had arrived safely home with the camper. And we hadn't received any letters from your father since leaving the States. You and Mike both cried about it. Since Athens, you'd written to Jack at least ten times. Jack hadn't sent you a single word. And I couldn't think of a single excuse for him.

I wrote home to my sister Bev and asked if she thought Jack would want one of you to live with him. I didn't know if Jack wanted to share in your lives, or if his new wife, Barbara, could handle children. I was concerned about your future, but I didn't know how to approach him and, obviously, I couldn't talk to you kids to find out what you wanted because your dad might not want you—a fear that turned out, as you know, to be valid.

The Girl in the Temple

On January 21, 1966, seven months into our world tour, we came to Banaras, India. By chance, we'd arrived on the most auspicious day of *Purna Kumbh Mela*, the Hindu bathing festival held once every twelve years.

My mother couldn't believe our luck—to have arrived in that particular place on that particular day, where pilgrims, walking for days, had come to take a dip in the holy Ganges. Relatives carried those who couldn't walk. Just three days before, we'd been in New Delhi on the same day Prime Minister Indira Gandhi was elected to office.

Soon after arriving at our "Tourist Hotel," Mike and I waited in the lobby while my mother argued with the turbaned man behind the counter. She wanted to see and experience the holiday firsthand and had asked the clerk to provide a driver and guide to take us to the river.

"It is too dangerous for American women and children," he told her. He was polite but firm, his bushy brows drawn together in an expression of disbelief. "The American consulate must have informed you."

While Mike wandered around the lobby handling the hotel's curios and decorations, I swung my legs under my chair and looked around. After sleeping in youth hostels or our Volkswagen van throughout Europe, inexpensive Near and Middle Eastern tourist hotels, with their tiled floors, rattan furniture, and floral wallpaper, seemed luxurious— except for their hole-in-the-floor, squat-over toilets, which I hated. The lobby sported large, faded pink flowers on textured, tan wallpaper and worn-looking, but clean, furniture—the same as our room. Tapestries of multi-armed, Hindu gods and goddesses adorned the walls. Mike gaped at a naked blue goddess wearing a necklace made of skulls. In her many hands, she held knives, an axe, a spear, a man's head, a bowl full of blood, and other objects I couldn't identify. Her eyes were wide and her tongue poked bright red from her mouth; I couldn't decide if her expression was mocking or defiant.

As Michael's hand reached upward, I hissed, "Stop touching things!" He turned, opened his eyes, stuck his tongue out at me in imitation of the blue goddess, and flattened his palm on the tapestry's border. Afraid he would get us both in trouble, I glanced at the man behind the counter. Embroiled in his argument with my mother, he hadn't noticed. I rolled my eyes and shrugged my shoulders.

"What's the point of traveling halfway around the world if we hide away in a hotel room?" my mother said, exasperated. "Just help me hire a driver and guide, that's all I'm asking."

"Madam—"

"Don't 'Madam' me," she said, seeming taller than five-foot-five-inches. "I want to speak to the manager."

"I *am* the manager." He spoke in an even tone, but his eyes flashed and his mouth formed a tight line between his black mustache and beard.

I'd seen this scenario before. My mother told me often enough that men in Asian and Middle Eastern countries weren't used to independent, outspoken women; all she had to do was yell, and eventually they would capitulate. If someone told my mother she couldn't do something, she would be even more determined to do it, and woe to the man who got in her way. I leaned back and watched Mike continue to make rounds of the room. The coffee table in the center of the lobby held a glass box containing a detailed, miniature replica of the Taj Mahal—to protect it from little boys, I thought.

Finally, the man said, "I will not be held responsible."

"Of course," she said, smiling. The manager picked up the phone and, within minutes, arrangements had been made for us to be picked up at the front of the hotel. My mother swept us up on her way out. "Quick, before he changes his mind."

It was winter in India—a cloudless blue sky greeted us as we passed through the lobby doors. Dust from the narrow dirt road drifted behind pilgrims headed toward the river. A confusion of color and motion and noise assailed my senses: men, wrapped in stained white sheets of cloth topped by jackets (I later learned they called their costume *dhoti* or *veshti*), laughing and talking and walking in groups; bangled women in colorful saris carrying children and baskets; babies crying; cars honking pedestrians out of their way; people calling and shouting to one another. I'd seen overcrowded streets during our previous days in Pakistan and India (we'd visited the Taj Mahal just the day before traveling to Banaras), but I'd not seen so many people and so much activity in one place. The tang of unwashed bodies mixed in the air with the rich scents of curries and incense, and the dust and the smoke of charcoal and dried dung fires.

Soon, a beat-up taxi pulled to the curb. A smiling, dark-skinned man, dressed in western-style khaki pants and a white cotton shirt unbuttoned at the collar, got out of the passenger's seat and introduced himself as our guide. He grinned and bobbed up and down as he spoke, which amused me. I couldn't help but return his smile. He assisted my mother to the passenger seat, motioned for Mike and me to get in behind her, then slid onto the back seat with us. He spoke a few words in Hindi and our taxi crept forward into the crowd. We made slow progress, as the driver kept having to honk his horn to get people to move out of our way. We stared at them and they stared at us as we passed, our windows rolled up against the dust and noise.

When my mother reached up to smash a mosquito against the windshield, the driver gasped and spoke in rapid, agitated Hindi.

"Hindus do not believe in killing other creatures, however small and insignificant," our guide explained when I asked why the driver had gotten upset. "It is the way of *ahimsa*, or non-violence."

My mother turned around in her seat. "Mosquitos carry disease—malaria and other horrible things," she said. "But these people believe in reincarnation. They think they might be born again as an insect or a monkey if they aren't good in this lifetime." Sensitive to how the man sitting next to me must feel, I squirmed inwardly. Our guide said nothing, but looked down at his hands, which lay on top of each other in his lap.

I stared at the red smear on the windshield and contemplated the idea of waking up one day as a mosquito. It seemed such a strange thing to believe, but I could understand why you'd be more careful how you treated other creatures. If I could be born again as a tree, it would be nice to be a redwood or an oak, to feel the warm sun on my rough bark and stretch out my branches for the birds to perch on.

About a mile from the river, we encountered a wall of people and could go no farther by car. "Are you sure, Madam, that you want to continue?" asked our guide.

My mother looked at the mass of bodies, seemed to hesitate for a moment. "Yes, I'm sure."

As we got out of the car, she grabbed our hands.

"You're hurting me," Mike said, grimacing. He tried to pull away, but she hauled us close and leaned over. "Hold my hands and don't let go. If we get separated in this crowd, I will never find you again. Never. Do you hear me?" Her voice was harsh and tight, and the veins throbbed on her neck.

I can still feel my mother's grasp, our palms pressed flat together, her heart beating a comforting, asynchronous rhythm against mine.

"The taxi will wait here," the guide said. "Please, do not take any pictures of beggars or cremations," as if my mother would let go of us to use her camera. "Follow me." Then he thrust forward through the crowd, pushing people aside to make room for us. I couldn't see beyond the swarming throng and watched with dismay as our guide disappeared between the curtains of saris and dhotis, abandoning us to the crowd. I suspect my mother, hurrying us after him, felt the same. I coughed as dust stirred by millions of feet rose into my face, filling my nostrils and stinging my eyes.

Beggars lined both sides of the street, propped against walls or along the gutters. Children as young as four or five, with infants perched on their laps, held their palms out, beseeching us with dark eyes. As we passed them, many displayed festering sores on small round cheeks or arms and legs. Flies swarmed the babies' eyes. Other beggars opened filthy scarves and head coverings to reveal missing noses and ears, or gashes where lips should have been. Some unwound dusty cloths from mangled limbs. An endless series of arms and hands reached out to us, tried to catch us, implored us for money.

I had seen plenty of begging during our travels, but it had never been like this. Mom had explained that beggars were frauds, feigning illness to win the sympathy of rich tourists; these did not seem like frauds to me. I shied away from them, horrified, fascinated, repelled, and bewildered by their poverty, their pain, and their silent accusations. Guilt for possessing a full stomach, clear skin, clean water, and a soft bed assailed me and brought tears to my eyes. I knew that even if we gave them all we had, it would only disappear into a black hole of need. Fearing we would be smothered by the supplicant mass of arms and legs, I pulled closer to my mother and grasped her forearm with my free hand.

"Mom, what's wrong with their faces?" Mike asked. His tone, a conflict of disgust and morbid interest, must have echoed my own. "Why are that woman's legs so big?"

My mother gestured toward a woman's disfigured face, "Leprosy." Toward the woman with legs as big around as small trees, "Elephantitis." At the children, "Infection. Stay close to me. Don't touch anything."

We turned off the main road and entered a marketplace—a wide dirt road narrowed by merchandise displayed in small, flimsy-looking booths or on carpets lying on the ground. A chaotic din of shouts, laughter, loud talking, women's high-pitched voices, and vendors hawking their wares surrounded us, but there were fewer people.

Vendors shouted as we passed, waving colorful fabrics, fruit, and cheap souvenirs. Some chased after us, demanding—angrily, it seemed to me—that we stop and buy their wares. This one would give us the best prices in all of Banaras. That one the highest quality mangos. Mike and I wanted to stop and look and touch, and asked ceaseless questions. We swiveled our heads from side to side, curious and frightened, trying to take it all in.

An emaciated cow, ribs outlined beneath its shabby hide, careened down the street like a giant tumbleweed, trampling products and pushing over carts. People moved out of its way, looking more irritated than alarmed. The vendors shouted at it and shoved it off their wares, then fixed their displays and continued peddling to the crowd.

"Mom, why do they let that cow just step all over everything?" I asked.

"Because the cow is sacred to the Hindus, and protected."

"It looks like it's starving. If it's sacred why don't they take care of it?" Mike wondered.

"They can't afford to feed it," she said.

We reached the end of the market and turned left into a slow river of cloth and feet. The world, with its crush of people, closed on me once again, and I clutched my mother's hand until I could no longer feel my fingertips. She towed us along, like a steamship parting the waves. Intent on following the dark little man in front of us, she wasn't stopping for anything.

After an interminable time, we arrived at the Ghats, the wide, stone steps leading to the river's edge. Over the sounds of shouts and general hubbub, we could hear singing and the rhythmic beat of ritual prayers.

"Here," our guide explained, "the pilgrims wait their turn to bathe in the Ganga, which will cleanse their souls and absolve them of sin. There are more than 100 Ghats in Banaras. It is the holiest of cities. That is why so many people come here for Purna Kumbh Mela. Now, we must hire a boat, so you can see."

We waited as he negotiated with a boatman at the bottom of the steps. He waved us down, and we climbed into a wide-bottomed boat, just large enough for the five of us. I sat with my mother on one of the two benches that spanned the center. Mike clambered up front, ignoring my mother's warnings to be careful. Our guide sat in back. The oarsman pushed away from the teeming shore, sprang into the boat next to our guide, and steered with his long pole toward the middle of the current and away from the throngs. The water surrounded and cushioned us from the noisy squall of humanity. As the chaos at the shoreline receded, I relaxed.

So many colorful figures swarmed the broad steps of the Ghats, I could barely see the stone beneath their feet. Balconied buildings rose behind the crowd in narrow bands of color—shades of brown, ochre, white, brick red, cherry red, yellow, and bright turquoise. Banners filled with ornate script stretched between buildings, and clothing thrown over the balconies' banisters fluttered in a light breeze.

The river itself was a murky, muddy brown. Men stripped to their loincloths and strode into the cold water, splashing it over their shoulders. Fully clothed women stood waist deep, their saris floating around them like colorful jellyfish. Some people immersed themselves neck deep in the water. Others splashed themselves ritually, dipping into the water with cupped hands, pouring it over their hair, and raising their arms in prayer. Some drank from their hands. We could see people clearing their nostrils into the water. One man brushed his teeth. As we moved downstream away from the Ghats, water buffalo, dogs, and cows mixed with the people in the water. Naked children played and urinated near their parents' ablutions.

Processions of grieving relatives bore shrouded bodies down the Ghats and placed them on top of funeral pyres, which burned close to the water's edge, their thick, gray smoke fanning out above us. Some of the processions were rich families. Bejeweled and wearing fine clothes, they carried their dead to the river on stretchers. Others were poor, their loved ones wrapped only in white cloth and lugged on the shoulders of two or three men. After placing the body on top of the pyre, someone would place a layer of wood on top of it—to keep the body from twisting off the pyre, our guide told us. Afterward, they disposed of the ashes into the water where, downstream, more pilgrims bathed and brushed their teeth. The wailing of women floated across the water to us from the shore, eerie and heartrending in its intensity.

Decomposing river weed, shoreline grasses, and fish always impart fetid smells to rivers, but the Ganges, full of human and cattle waste, emitted a sewer-like odor. Remembering the sick beggars we'd passed, I asked, "Mom, why are they *drinking* the dirty water?"

"They believe the river is sacred and has healing powers. It's part of their religion," she said.

After that, we remained silent for a while, drifting with the current away from the crush.

As we continued downstream, the Ghats and the crowds thinned. Noise came from behind rather than on all sides, and we began to see stands of trees. Little by little, the sandy beaches gave way to lush green riverbanks, and buildings and crowds gave way to jungle. The air thickened with the sounds of birds and chattering monkeys. Mike, who had been uncharacteristically quiet, pointed and laughed at the monkeys—hundreds of them, jumping from branch to branch of the trees along the shore. If we came too close, they screeched, threw small objects at us, and shook their fists. Mike was enchanted, but I shrank back from their rage and their pointy teeth, glad we were safe in the middle of the river.

As we rounded a long, smooth bend, the river narrowed. The trees bowed gracefully over us, creating an emerald archway mirrored in the ripples our boat made as it sliced through the water. Though I could have thrown a stone onto the riverbank, I almost didn't see the temple hidden by the foliage. It might have been a flash of gold from the slender, domed roof or a glimpse of the cherry red paint that caught my attention.

"Mommy, look at that," I said, pointing. I could see it better now, perched on the edge of land above the river. Beneath it, the bank cut a steep mud wall where fernlike plants sprouted through tangles of roots and stones. Intricate designs adorned every surface of the temple, and jeweled ornaments hung from the balustrade of a second floor balcony facing the river. As I gazed at the balcony, a girl about my age moved into view.

Her bejeweled and sequined sari sparkled in the sun, which winked through the leafy canopy in thin, sharp rays, making everything about her glitter like a fairytale character come to life. My breath caught and my mouth gaped open. She must be a princess, I thought. Or, maybe, a real live goddess!

She placed her small, pale hands on the railing, leaned over, and gazed into the water. Points of light from what looked like tiny, encrusted diamonds, sprung from her gleaming red fingernails. Gold bangles covered her arms, and gold and pearl earrings flashed from her earlobes. She wore eye shadow in bright shades of blue and green, and her cheeks were sculpted with rouge. I saw her as elegant and perfect, with an exquisite beauty befitting a princess.

Time and motion suspended while I, aware of no sound except the swish of my quickened heartbeat, stared at the girl on the balcony.

As if drawn by the intensity of my wonder, she lifted her gaze and stared at me. I don't know what I expected to see—mirth, or perhaps haughtiness—but not those dead, black eyes. I had imagined her important and proud; now, I could see her slumped shoulders and turned-down mouth. The sight pierced my heart and weighed me down, crushing some profound hope I couldn't have named and didn't know I held. I wanted to cry.

"Mommy," I whispered, my eyes still locked with the girl's, "who is that, and why is she so sad?"

"She's a temple prostitute," my mother said. "She's not allowed to leave the temple."

Though I was just ten, I'd seen prostitutes on the streets in Italy and Amsterdam and knew, in general terms, what they did. I pictured this beautiful little girl in the company of the fat, old men who brought offerings to the temple.

I thought about the stacks of fairytale books and stories on my nightstand at home, with their princesses and kings, magicians and heroes. I thought what it would be like never to play with other children, never to *be* a child, only a prisoner. A gilded songbird locked in a cage with no hope of escape. No fair prince or night enchantments to free me.

It was as if I were the one standing on that balcony with the gilded temple prison at my back while a little white girl, rich and beautiful—and free—floated by.

As the boat drifted past, I turned. The girl in the temple and I followed each other with our eyes and, just before she disappeared from view, I thought I saw her lift a small, pale hand in farewell.

✦

JACKIE

I often wondered what to make of all those experiences and felt anxious wondering how I could capture them. My little insignificant notes, mountains of them that I carried with me around the world, didn't make any sense.

I had been unprepared for my emotional response to the Taj Mahal— skin chilled, throat constricted, eyes filled with tears. No intellectual or verbal explanation can describe my body's reaction to the viewing of this architectural wonder—a sort of mysterious, lyrical beauty, unequalled by any building I'd ever seen. Inside, beneath the central dome where light filtered through a double screen of perforated marble lay buried, side by side in ornate tombs, the Emperor and his wife. Exquisite designs inlaid with semi-precious stones covered the walls.

And when we came to Banaras, India, I couldn't believe we'd arrived on the most important religious holiday in twelve years. I remember how frightened I was of being separated from you as we made our way down to the river with our guide. After we broke our way through the crowd for about three quarters of a mile, a wooden post separated Mike from me and his hand slipped out of mine. I screamed louder than any scream I had made before. Time stopped. Even the crowd seemed to stop. Then Mike found my hand again on the other side of the post. At that point, even had I wanted to, there was no going back—we had to push forward to the river.

When we finally made it into the boat, I felt so relieved. We could see everything from there: the water oxen and all kinds of animals, the masses of people on the shore and bathing in the river, and the funeral pyres. The guide told me the dead bodies wrapped in red were women. Widows and men were wrapped in white. They burned fourteen bodies at once to save time: it took three hours. The bereaved set the fires then sat moaning and crying by the burning bodies for hours until they could dump the ashes into the Ganges. The mourners' chanting and crying made me want to cry too.

Although it was more than two hours before we returned to our taxi, I don't remember walking back.

At night, I'd lay awake worrying about what your lives would be like when we returned home. I had resigned myself to the fact that your father wouldn't want any of you. And what would I do about my freedom? Private schools are more acceptable than having children live with other families, but the cost of boarding schools for you youngest three would have been prohibitive. I thought if I lived in the apartment over the garage, maybe I'd be able get a couple for the house who would help take care of you.

Then I would think about all the children in those primitive countries—millions of babies—often deformed and sickly. In India, the life span was only forty years. Life on this earth just didn't make any sense.

There was so much searching within me. How long would it take to get it out of my system?

Carr Family, 1957

Jackie and Jack

Yew Street house in winter

Mike and I, 1962

Mother-daughter dresses

Teen counseling "rap" session
John, far left, age 15

Leaving for our world tour, June 1965

At the Parthenon

*Celso's musical group and note
to Jackie*

*Hosni & child performer with me
in Egyptian desert nightclub*

The Taj Mahal

Crowded bridge over Ganges River
during Purna Kumbh Mela

PART TWO

Attack Therapy

My brother John picked us up from the San Francisco Airport in our blue Volkswagen camper—the same one we'd lived in all over Europe and shipped home from Greece. It felt strange riding in it again, our luggage piled on top of the bed in back. As we drove home, I fingered the silver charms on my bracelet. The small, silver pendants fluttered against the tips of my fingers, and images floated before my eyes like ghosts. The oh-so-green of Ireland. Mushroom hunting in the woods outside Barcelona. The ribbon thin, winding roads in the Pyrenees Mountains. The Colosseum, the Parthenon, and the Taj Mahal. It seemed both like yesterday and a hundred years ago that we'd left home for our trip around the world, like a fading dream.

Mike sat across from me, the Formica-topped, folding table between us. I was on the short seat next to the sink, my back to John. How would it be when we got home? So much had happened before we left: the fights, the divorce, Dad's moving. Richard had come to Japan while we were there and would not be returning until the end of summer. Terry was at UCLA. I wasn't sure about John. Would he be living with us or going away to college?

I tried to listen to his conversation with Mom in the front of the van, but the loud *putt-putt-putting* of the engine obscured their words. Mom had had to repossess our house while we were away, because the buyer didn't make his payments, and she was going on about it. I could make out snatches of her side of the conversation: "Default ... bank ... summer ... your father ..."

"Mom?" I called over my left shoulder. She didn't look up, so I tried again, a little louder. "Mom?" Still no response. "Mom!" She glanced at me but kept talking to John. I could see him eyeing me in the rear view mirror, an amused glint in his blue eyes. I sighed and gave up.

Mike mocked me. "Linda? ... Linda? ... Linda! ..." his voice rising with each repetition of my name. I knew as soon as I said, "What?" he'd say, "That's what," so I ignored him. He stuck his tongue out, and I stuck mine out right back. But then he started making stupid faces at me. I sighed. It would be a relief not to be cooped up in a car or an airplane with Mike.

I turned my face to the window. Though all the streets and buildings were the same, they all looked different. The stores were gigantic. The streets, lined with tall shade trees, sidewalks, and landscaped parking strips, all watered and green, appeared more lush than I remembered, and I wondered if the house I was returning to would also seem larger than before.

At the beginning of summer, Mom sold our house a second time and we moved to a rented, three-bedroom duplex in Redwood City, one-third the size of our house in San Mateo. It sat on a corner, the front door facing one street and the garage the other. A straight, concrete walkway, with a tiny, rectangular patch of lawn on either side of it, led from the sidewalk to the front door. Our new neighborhood was quiet. All the houses had tidy bits of lawn like ours, and children played in yards and rode bicycles in the cul-de-sacs. My new room was a convert-ed carport, separated from the rest of the household by the kitchen and laundry room. A place to which I could escape—dark and quiet and pri-vate—a place I could curl in on myself.

To meet men, Mom began working nights as a first-class escort. ("Just escort—no 'extra'—services," she said.) She also rented a post office box and placed personal ads in the paper. Sometimes she shared the responses with me.

"What do you think, should I go out with this one?" The letter would be accompanied by a picture of a man in a striped bathing suit, muscles flexed in a classic Jack LaLanne pose. I'd wrinkle my nose and shake my head. My mother would laugh, but she'd write him back. She wrote them all back.

I spent most of that summer indoors with the blinds drawn, watching cartoons, game shows, and soap operas. If I had known what I was feeling, I might have said that I felt lonely and a little scared. I had no friends, and I'd be starting junior high school in the fall as an outsider. I might have said that I missed the closeness my mother and I shared while traveling, missed how, when we walked down the cobblestone streets holding hands, she'd squeeze my hand three times. It was our secret signal: squeeze-squeeze-squeeze, I-love-you. But now, all my brothers except Mike were away, and my mother, occupied with other things, was rarely home. A vague seed-ache of abandonment took root in me and began to grow. It seems to me now that this must be when the Tar began oozing its way into my heart.

My mother's letters explain what I couldn't understand then: all the things she did—attending transpersonal development workshops, experimenting with LSD and marijuana, dating, and traveling—intoxicated her. She'd freed herself from the constraints of marriage, and she also longed to be free from mothering. She wrote Terry,

> I seem to be at war with the fear of being "possessed," even by the kids. It feels like I'm in deep water, trying to live, and I have to beat the kids off or be pulled under. If I can find students, someone, something to take over part of my 'job,' maybe I can find some peace. ... I keep saying, "When I'm really single, I'm going to do all sorts of things and live in a small place alone." I crave aloneness.

As I read my mother's words now, my stomach tightens. I remember saying the same things when I was a single mother with two grown and two young children at home—about the same age my mother was when she wrote to Terry. I remember the first time I managed to go away for a weekend by myself—I was forty-three—and how I came back determined to carve out time in my life just for me. Remembering how alone and abandoned and hurt I felt when my mother began to spread her wings, I wonder now how my children felt when I began to spread mine.

When I think back to that year in that duplex in Redwood City, I see shades of brown and colorless shadow: oatmeal shag carpets, a burnt-sienna couch with beige cushions, pale ecru drapes pulled shut, the tan walls in the living room, wood doors, and the darker wood paneling in my bedroom. Colors my mother thought were easy to clean and wouldn't show dirt.

I'd walk in the door after school, shouting "Hello!" into those brown shadows. Sometimes Mike was home, sometimes not. Sometimes Richard would be in his room with one or more of his friends, door shut, the music from his portable record player drowning out the sounds of boys laughing. Mom would come home later, after teaching a night class or after a date.

So I'd arrive home to Mrs. C, the housekeeper, a heavy, older woman my mother hired to babysit us and heat our TV dinners (she didn't actually clean the house). A closet drinker, she moved stiffly and slowly, as though life itself was an imposition.

She would lurk in the doorway between the bedroom hall and the living room, wearing her faded blue, flowered housedress. A frown creased her face while she watched us, her big, flabby arms crossed over her chest while she barked commands, the effort squeezing the breath out of her like an old dog, too tired to get up from her post to route intruders.

One day—I'm not sure what started the argument—she growled at me with more than her usual energy as she wobbled at her post. I was eating in the living room (perhaps that was the problem), and I threw a butter knife in her direction, aiming it low so that it bounced off the baseboard. I didn't intend to hurt her, but to scare her. It worked, and she retreated into her room, leaving me alone.

Later, when my mother came home, the housekeeper told her I tried to kill her with a butcher knife. I laughed at the bizarre idea that anyone would believe that old drunk.

Mike, Richard, and I fought—a lot. On a Saturday when Mom wasn't home, the two of them held me down while Richard stuffed ice cubes in my training bra. I squirmed and cried as the ice burned cold against my nipples. They laughed and teased me about not having any breasts while I sobbed with shame and humiliation. When all the ice melted, they let me go.

I had my usual ways of getting even. I'd trash their bedrooms, pull clothes out of their drawers and throw them around the room, knock books and toys off shelves onto the floor—then hide behind my locked bedroom door.

But retribution always came, sooner or later, and there was no place I felt safe.

Mom told us her students made her feel loved, accepted, and cared for, and that teaching filled her with energy. Her study hall class was always full, and she had overheard kids whispering in the cafeteria that she was the "cool" teacher. And she advocated for her students when they got into trouble.

When we'd lived in San Mateo, she'd held "rap sessions" at the house. Her students would sit in a circle and talk about their lives while my mother listened and gave them advice. But the students didn't come to this house, so far away from Hillsdale High School, and I didn't like being compared to them. It felt as though being her child was less important than being her student.

When Mom *was* home she was writing. Or she was tired. Mike and Richard and I would squabble with one another, until she'd scream in frustration, "Why can't you be like my students?"

"Because they don't have to live with you!" I would scream back, hating every one of those mindless, teacher-worshipping students.

Tar.

One night, as I sat on the floor of the living room watching "Bewitched," Mom snuck up behind me and cut off my ponytail with a pair of kitchen shears. I screamed.

"What's wrong with you?" she wanted to know.

"Wrong? You just cut off my hair!" I held what was left of it in my hands. "I was trying to grow it out. I don't *want* short hair! I *hate* you!" I ran to my room, slamming the door twice for good measure, locked it, threw myself on the bed and buried my face in my pillow, crying and screaming. "I hate you! I hate you! ... You're not my real mother!" I pounded my pillow. I wanted to run away, but there was nowhere to go.

My hair had *finally* grown long enough to stuff into a stubby little ponytail. Every night I counted brush strokes, because I read in a magazine that brushing at least one-hundred strokes every day would make your hair silkier and grow faster. Now, it would be shorter than ever.

I went to the mirror and stared at myself. Angry, hazel eyes stared back at me from red, puffy cheeks and swollen eyelids, and my breath dragged through my sore throat in ragged gulps. She hadn't even cut my hair straight; it slanted crazily from my earlobe on the right side to the midline of my jaw on the left. I imagined everyone at school standing around me in a circle, pointing their fingers and laughing. I closed my eyes. Red pulsed behind my lids. "Please don't let this be real," I whispered. "Please … please …" But when I opened my eyes it was real. There was no way I could go to school the next day with hair like that. I had no choice but to let her "fix" it.

I went to find my mother. She sat at the desk in her bedroom, typing a letter to my brother John.

"Mom," I said.

She looked up. "What's wrong with it?"

"It's crooked, can't you see?" My fingers grasped the ends of my hair on both sides of my face.

"Okay, come on." She led me into the kitchen, spread newspapers on the floor, pulled a chair from the table, and placed it on top of the newspaper. I sat down, beaten.

"You look so much nicer with short hair," she said. She clipped the left side. I winced. "Sit up straight," she said, "and stop wiggling."

When she had cut the sides and back level, she said, "Let me cut your bangs, too. They're hanging in your eyes. I don't know how you can see." She didn't wait for my answer, but began snipping.

"There! Isn't that nice?" she said, and held up a small hand mirror. I peered into it. I looked like someone had put a bowl over my head before cutting my hair. Stony-faced, I got up from the chair and walked back to my room, not sure how I would live through the next day.

My mother never understood why I got so upset. In that letter to John, she wrote,

> Do you know that it's a major war these days to get kids to cut their hair? … Linda cried for an hour because I took off one inch, plus the part of her bangs that was hanging in her eyes. Boy, I wish kids could get back their perspective about what's important.

Sometimes when I came home from school, Mom, Rick, and Mike would be waiting for me, four folding chairs placed in a small circle in the living room. Mom had learned about "encounter groups" during her personal growth workshops at Synanon. This group therapy, which would later be dubbed "attack therapy" by psychologists, used personal confrontation and ridicule to break down participants' defenses and—so its proponents claimed—heal core hurts. In that circle, we were encouraged to express our rage and belittle one another, as my mother facilitated. Our only rules were to stay in our chairs and not touch each other.

Mom believed she was helping us develop as emotionally healthy individuals, but during those sessions, we said horrible, bitter things to each other, and I always left the circle feeling worse than when I sat down.

One day, when I walked through the front door and saw those hateful chairs circled and waiting, I groaned. It had been a hard day at school. The girls all talked about me behind their hands, giggling, and two of them hit me as I walked by them in the hallway. Still, I knew if they ever extended any kindness toward me, I'd drop everything and lick their hands, like a puppy. Just the thought of my weak desire for their approval made my stomach clench. Now, a darkness of self-loathing roiled in me, a scouring hurt that made me feel scraped and raw. So when I saw the chairs, I wanted to run away. I wanted to curl up in my mother's lap like a baby and be rocked into oblivion.

A sliver of light slid into the room where the closed drapes didn't quite meet, illuminating the shadows and a band of dust motes. I watched the motes stir and swirl in the current our bodies made as we moved into our chairs.

Mom began, "Tell Linda what bothers you about her."

I braced myself, determined not to let them hurt me.

"You think you're smart, little Goody Two Shoes, always the *good* girl."

"You talk too much."

"You get your own room and all the attention, I hate you."

"You're ugly. You're fat and you have a big nose."

"You yell at me and won't share."

"You don't have any friends because no one wants to be seen with you."

"I hate you because you get everything you want. You're not even my real sister, only my half sister."

And so on. I imagined their words leaping from their mouths and falling to the floor, where they wriggled like spiders. I *wouldn't* let them see how I felt. I struck out, harsh in my desire to draw blood and appease the darkness within me.

To Mike: "You're stupid. You can't read. You even *look* retarded with those gigantic ears, like Dumbo the elephant, ready to fly away. It's because of *you* I don't have any friends. You can't even tie your shoes and you still wet your bed."

To Richard: "You're lazy and fat. You don't know how to do anything. You think you're a big shot, but you're nothing but a coward. I detest you because you hit me and pick on me. All you care about is your friends and trying to get girls. You can barely read or write. You're as dumb as Mike."

It was a typical encounter session.

After Mike and I cried and we had all calmed down, my mother surprised me by asking, "Linda, would you ever smoke marijuana?"

She still didn't know that I smoked cigarettes. I hadn't thought much about marijuana and shrugged. "Maybe. Just to try it."

"Okay, Rick," she said, and looked meaningfully at my brother, who led me into his bedroom where he proceeded to stuff a pipe full of small green leaves from a plastic bag. He lit it and instructed me to inhale and hold the smoke in for as long as possible. He filled the pipe again, and I managed to inhale the smoke a couple more times.

Returning to the living room, I sat on the couch and studied my family. The thought that my own mother was the one to introduce me to pot made me giggle. My head felt heavy and dropped to the side as if it was not attached to my shoulders. This made me giggle some more. My mother's nonplussed expression and my brothers' curious stares, as if I were an animal in the zoo, caused me to laugh even more. Finally, when my mother got tired of my uncontrollable giggling, she gave me two aspirin and put me to bed.

JACKIE

Life after returning home from our trip around the world was filled with the ugly business of finances, straightening up my affairs, and the boredom of daily living. I put the house up for sale a second time, began apartment hunting, and found the duplex in Redwood City. I also put an ad in the paper for live-in help; I wanted someone at home so I could be free to go when I wanted to.

Over the summer I tried LSD once, and marijuana. But neither of them had much effect on me. (I always needed to control situations and, even under the influence of drugs, I was in control.) I traveled a little around California and went to Alaska with the boyfriend I called "Old Faithful." I'd known him for two years and he was devoted, but I couldn't match his feelings.

And I couldn't seem to find any one man that I felt compatible with. Old Faithful stood by ready, willing, and able to do anything for me. But he bored me. I had one boyfriend who excited me, but I could only take him in small doses and felt threatened if he was around for more than a couple of days at a time. It frightened me when men wanted to usurp too much of my time, effort, or energy. I guess after my marriage and the kids, I didn't want to take care of anyone else.

I was so tired of all the responsibility with you kids. Not that I hadn't always had it anyway, but without your dad's help, it was never-ending. I really enjoyed my children; every one of you was planned and wanted. But you, Richard, and Mike sure fought with each other. There were times I just wanted to send you all away to boarding schools and have peace for myself.

In spite of the fighting, I wasn't concerned about you, Linda. You were, as always, at the top of your class, and at eleven strong enough to turn me off when you needed to. You were overly sensitive, got impatient (now where the hell did you learn that?), and wanted to be perfect, but I didn't worry. You didn't cause any troubles or concern; you were almost a non-entity in the family, so I didn't think we needed to pay attention to you.

The hard part of being a mother, for me, was that I internalized everything. When you kids were little and you had an earache, I had an earache, and when one of you hit the other, I felt I was being hit. Then as you kids grew up, and when you were emotionally hurt or lost, I felt that hurt and loss as if it were my own, sometimes so strongly that I could hardly function.

When John was court-martialed for refusing to fight in the war, I sometimes thought it was more painful for me than for him—but I didn't really believe that. I was proud of him. I couldn't have taken his stand—I always had too great a fear of authority. During the time waiting for him to be drafted and then, later, waiting for his sentencing, I became increasingly "authority anxious." I had trouble sleeping, and when I slept I had nightmares. I felt ineffective, impotent, and helpless as if we were being "done unto."

But I was so steeped in the excitement of my own life, sometimes it was as though I didn't know what day it was or where I was. With artwork, Bridge Mountain Foundation, LSD, marijuana, Esalen Institute, writing, reading, people, you kids, the house, a class at the free University of Palo Alto, training for the Peninsula Suicide Prevention Hotline, students visiting, dates with men, plus moving, all in the first three months after we returned home, my life was *full*.

The thing that scared me was that I couldn't seem to set limits. How many people did I have to be important to? I had five or six men at a time phoning for dates, and I didn't want to say no to anyone, even a likable truck driver who was so humble he asked, "Would an invitation for dinner get a rejection?"

I thought maybe I could be important on a larger scale, not only through writing but in connection with something "big." For instance, I went to the Western Behavior Science Institute in La Jolla and had lunch with Richard

Farson, the president, and he invited me to a staff meeting with Carl Rogers. These were important people. And I knew if I were a climber, I could make it. Then Eric Berne, who wrote several books, including Games People Play, *was also interested in me. But I wasn't the aggressive type, and who says that Eric Berne as a human being is more valuable than a truck driver?*

I used to feel I had no choice, that life ran me, that I had to live my life as it was set up. When and how did I learn I could make choices? Maybe it was somewhere around the time I took the most dangerous and devastating step of all—that terrifying choice to be divorced. It took great courage to leave the secure world and go out into the unknown to find what was there.

I learned, because I believed in people in general, to believe in the choices I made for myself. They felt right. I believed in the essence of each person, that each human has the capacity for good, although many—maybe most— don't achieve goodness much of the time.

What is the best part of life? Perhaps feelings are the best part: strong, overwhelming passions that take control of one's whole being. And perhaps the longing for love is the strongest. Love brings ecstasy, so great I sometimes felt I would be willing to sacrifice all the rest of life for a few hours of that kind of joy; love erases loneliness, that shivering, cold lifeless place where one stands defenseless; and finally, in the union of love with another is the mystery of life—what the poets and the great artists imagine. I was fortunate in life to find this kind of love.

I also had a passion for knowledge. I wanted to know everything, to understand what makes human beings do what they do and to know why we function and how and what we can achieve.

Together, love and knowledge sent me upward into the heavens and gave me the high points of my life.

Summer Flight

In October of 1966, when my mother began flying lessons, it seemed as if it was all she talked about: "It's the most thrilling, magnificent experience!" And when she passed the exam for her pilot's license the following March, we threw a party for her. Bill (Old Faithful) brought a cake. As though it were her birthday, we dished out ice cream, lit candles, and sang, "Happy Flying to You." Mom's eyes sparkled as she clapped her hands and laughed.

In spite of the freedom and excitement about life she'd experienced since her divorce from Dad, Mom began talking about running away for a while. "I need a break from everything," she announced, along with her decision to take Mike and me on a summer flying tour of the United States.

Remembering how close my mother and I had been while traveling around the world, I looked forward to having her nearly all to myself once again.

She set a goal of touching down in all 48 contiguous states, as well as visiting my brother John, who had been sentenced to two years at Fort Leavenworth Prison. He was drafted in September, but in boot camp he put down his gun and refused to pick it up again. He realized, he said, that he would not be able to kill another person; he was a Conscientious Objector.

In preparation for our trip, Mom brought Mike and me along on practice flights, taught me how to read navigation maps (she said I would be her co-pilot), and showed Mike how to spot landmarks. It felt good to have the three of us together, traveling again, as though we'd gone back in time and I could bask once again in my mother's constant love and attention.

Mom contacted news agencies and sent query letters to magazine publishers. She researched routes, weather patterns, and flew several times per week. She made arrangements for Rick's room and board, for someone to take care of the house while we were gone, and placed ads in the classified sections of local newspapers in every state we'd be visiting:

```
Attractive female pilot, accompanied by son (10),
daughter (12) flying 48 states. Desires regional
hosts or guides. Respond to Box #.
```

All along our way, newspaper reporters, officials from hotels, aviation companies, the airplane manufacturers that sponsored us, and people interested in such an unusual family would meet us for interviews and pictures.

On Friday, June 16, 1967, we posed for local reporters, standing proudly next to our Piper Cherokee. In the photograph my mother looks trim in her brown leather flight jacket and short wavy hair; I, prepubescent and awkward, stand close, seeming to emulate her confidence; and Mike, in jeans and a short-sleeved, button-down shirt, scowls against the sun.

Then we climbed into our rented plane and waved goodbye to all that had been troubling us at home.

Fifteen minutes into what should have been a twenty-minute flight from Denver to Colorado Springs, dark clouds swirled and swelled with alarming velocity into thick, threatening towers behind our one-engine

Cherokee Piper. We'd spent the morning with representatives from Jeppeson, an aviation map company. At their office, photographers snapped pictures of my mother, Mike, and me looking at maps with the company's vice president, and the publicity had pushed our planned, early morning takeoff to mid-afternoon. And when my mother pulled back the wheel to lift our plane off the tarmac, the sky had been clear except for a few high, scattered clouds.

Now, enormous thunderclouds rushed forward and wrapped them-selves around our little plane. In an instant, the sky went so black we could barely see the tips of our wings. Icy rain and hail pounded against the windshield, while winds and pressure changes caused us to drop and rise and shake. It was like riding an elevator gone crazy. My stomach flip-flopped with each movement, and bile burned the back of my throat.

Jagged knives of lightning pierced the darkness on both sides of us, accompanied by explosions of thunder. I could feel the hair standing out from my neck and arms, could taste the rain and something like burnt metal. Each time a bolt sliced the sky, we pitched sideways. Veins stood out like blue cords on the backs of my mother's hands as she fought to maintain control of the plane, which rocked from side to side like a toy in the hands of a great, malevolent monster.

When a burst from the clouds caused us to hurtle sideways, I screamed and covered my ears, picturing us ripped to pieces and scat-tered over the landscape below. In the seat behind me, Mike was either yelling or laughing maniacally; I couldn't tell which for all the din around us.

Gripping the wheel with her left hand, my mother wrestled the mi-crophone free with the other and radioed the tower in Colorado Springs. "Would you like us to guide you in by instruments?" they asked.

"No, I can't!" Mom replied, voice shaking. She didn't explain that she had earned her pilot's license just two months before and didn't know how to make an instrument landing. It was all she could do to hold the plane level. We dipped again. She dropped the microphone on the floor by my feet.

"We're going to outrun it," she said. Aiming the nose of the plane toward a thin gray line on the horizon, she pushed the Cherokee as fast as it would go—125 miles per hour. But the storm howled and clamped its jaws around us.

"Look for a place to land," my mother yelled over the roar of the wind and rain. "A field, a road, anything!" Her arms strained and trembled as she continued to fight the wheel, which jerked and turned against her. Mike and I squinted through the thick rivulets streaming across our windows and into the darkness below. Every once in a while, one of us would make out the faint outlines of fences, the green and yellow of fields thick with corn. We had been flying for over two hours and had no idea where we were.

Then I heard my mother whisper, "Dear God, please don't let my children die! I'll do anything, just let us get through this."

I turned and stared at her open-mouthed. She didn't believe in God. Hearing her pray terrified me more than anything that had happened so far. Being in control had always been so important to my mother, she defied fear, attacking whatever threatened or tried to hold her back. And, as far as I knew, she always won. I had never heard her plead in any of the risky situations we'd been in during our travels around the world two years before. If my mother didn't know how to get out of this situation, then no one did, and we might really die. The fear coiling around my chest squeezed tighter.

"Look!" Mike yelled, pointing. Below us was a small airstrip with a red-roofed hanger and a few planes.

On our first and second approaches, the wind blew us too far right. At the last moment, Mom pulled the wheel back. The wings shuddered with effort, lifting the plane into the air again. On the third try, my mother approached as if we were planning to land on the gravel to the left of the runway. We were blown in line and touched down. The plane rocked and bounced, threatening to veer off into the muddy ruts of a plowed field, but we were on the ground! We taxied to a tie-down spot, pushed open the doors, and struggled to hook the chains to the wings with our small hands. Rain drenched us and the wind pulled at our clothes and hair.

We grabbed our shared overnight case and ran to the small airport office. It was closed, so we walked to the country road that fronted the airport—empty as far as we could see—and waited. After a time, a battered red and white truck approached. We stuck out our thumbs.

The truck stopped and a middle-aged man with a weathered face rolled down the window. "Climb in," he said. The three of us crammed into the front seat, water draining from us onto the floorboards and into the upholstery.

"I saw you come down," he said, "thought you might be in some trouble and came to take a look."

That was just about the nicest thing I'd ever heard. Mom explained what had happened. The man told us we were still in Colorado, in Las Animas about 125 miles southeast of Colorado Springs, and drove us to the nearest motel. All I wanted was a hot shower, dry clothing, and to feel the ground underneath my feet.

Getting ready for bed that night Mike teased me about being afraid. Holding his head in his hands and rolling his eyes up so that all we could see were the whites, "Aaah! Aaah!" he wailed. "We're going to die! We're going to die!"

I threw a pillow at him. "You were scared too, you little liar!" But I started to laugh, because he was right, and because it all seemed so funny now that we were safe on the ground.

Mom laughed, too, but when I tried to tease her about praying, she said, "I did not!" Her still trembling hands betrayed her, but the denial comforted me: it felt like the mother I believed in had returned, and that mother would never admit she'd been scared enough to pray.

We hopped from state to state like grasshoppers, rarely staying more than a day or two in one place. Cooped up in our cockpit, as small as the inside of a Volkswagen bug, we often flew for five hours at a time. So much of our summer was spent in that tiny space that, to this day, I find the aroma of a new car—very much like the Cherokee's interior leather-seat-smell—repulsive. It was noisy too; at the end of a long trip, our ear-drums continued to vibrate for hours. If we wanted to talk, we had to yell over the roar of the engine, so we spoke only when needed for take-off, navigation, and landing. My mother flew "out loud." By that, I mean that she would speak our altitude and bearings every time she checked them, and then she'd ask me to point out where we were on the map.

"Keep a lookout for other planes," she would shout to both of us. "We need to keep our distance … and birds. Watch for flocks of birds." Birds could be devastating to small planes.

Mike would get bored, and it seemed to me that he was always scowling, never happy no matter what we did. If I was in front, he would soon begin kicking the back of my seat or poking me in the side. I would yell at him, Mom would yell at both of us, and Mike would sit back with a satisfied look on his face, only to begin again as soon as I'd gotten immersed in a map or spellbound watching the land glide be-neath us. Mom liked it when I was the undemanding "mature one," so as much as possible I volunteered to sit in back and let Mike co-pilot; be-sides, I could navigate just as well from there.

The first time we flew for more than three hours straight, it shocked me when my mother produced a small jar, pulled her pants down, peed in it, and proceeded to pour it out the tiny triangle-shaped wing vent. I pictured the fine, golden mist descending on plants, animals, and people, and wrinkled my nose. "Mom," I said, "Eeeeuuwwww."

"What else am I supposed to do?" she asked, her eyebrows arched at me.

Mike, in the co-pilot's seat, giggled.

"Fine. You just go ahead and laugh," Mom said, the corners of her mouth twitching, "but you won't be able to hold it when you get older, either." Mike and I always refused to use the jar no matter how badly we had to pee.

In Florida, we landed at a not-yet-completed resort on Marco Island, which my mother remarked was "out in the boonies" and "smells like insect repellent." The resort owners had offered to put us up for a couple of days in one of their luxury villas in return for local publicity and my mother's promise to write an article for an industry magazine.

As my mother toured the resort with the owners and later holed up in our villa to write, Mike and I wandered the nearly empty resort. On the beach, palm trees bordered the white sand that stretched, like glittering ribbons, on either side of me as I faced the turquoise water.

Mike and I chased the waves, bodysurfed, and collected shells. He spent hours digging in the sand, throwing rocks into the water, or running up and down the beach scaring the birds. Sometimes I joined him. It felt wonderful to move our bodies after flying for so long, and we played together as though we were little again.

In the afternoon, I went to the beach by myself and swam in the embracing warmth of the Gulf, watched the eggplant purple sky break open in the distance, jagged slices of light reaching down like fingers to touch the water. I was alone on the beach. I knew I should come in out of the impending storm, but the electrical charge in the air and the wildness of the wind exhilarated me.

I shared my mother's love of adventure, the heart-pounding adrenalin rush of risk. And yet at that moment, I also became aware of a difference between us: Mom was all intellect and movement, achievement and growth, never standing still, never acknowledging anything larger than herself (excepting that one time during the storm). Standing on that white-sand, Florida beach, I felt an all-encompassing presence and an inner quiet. I thought my mother would scoff at these feelings, so I kept them to myself.

In Miami, my mother placed Mike and me with a family for a week while she traveled to Puerto Rico and the Caribbean islands with Bill. Through her letters, I learn that throughout the summer, Bill or Joe—the one she was excited about at the time—would fly out and tour with us. Often, as I read her account of our trip, buried memories dislodge and float to the surface. But I have no memory, whatsoever, of Joe or Bill having been with us. I remember the family, and the giant Florida cockroaches, but not why my mother left us there or where she went.

What strange mechanism of the mind causes me to remember one thing and not another? Perhaps I blocked these men from memory because I wanted it to be just my mother, my little brother, and me, and resented sharing her with anyone else. Perhaps it was simply that my young mind was focused on its own, self-centered perceptions. Probably, I didn't consider those men important. At a young age I had learned that men leave. Brothers leave. I could let them all go.

After Mom returned from the Caribbean, we flew to Fort Lauderdale, where a man at Red Aircraft Service, another one of our sponsors, supplied us with over-water survival equipment and helped us get special clearance from the FAA to fly to Nassau in the Bahamas—one of my mother's flying goals.

"You have to wear life jackets for the entire trip," the man told us, "and you need to carry and know how to use a life raft." He showed us how to ditch the plane and how to inflate the raft while in the water.

Then we took off and headed straight out over the ocean. After a half hour, we were beyond radio contact. We could see nothing but water on all sides and had nothing to guide us but our compass. Sitting in the back, I pressed my nose against the window and watched the shadowy forms at the bottom of the turquoise sea.

In Nassau, they made us empty out the plane and go through customs. Mike, because he was smallest and that was his job, climbed into the tail of the plane and handed out the luggage. In the hotel room, Mom paced and fretted and planned, so nervous about the return flight over the water that she couldn't relax. We would stay for one night, she said. Mike and I begged to stay longer and play on the beach, but Mom got up before dawn and packed all our things so we could leave right after breakfast.

It was more important to my mother that we touch down in every place she'd mapped on the itinerary than that we experience those places. It was always that way. Life was a smorgasbord: she tasted everything on the table, but rarely paused to enjoy what she was eating.

"When I grow up and travel, I'm going to stay long enough to enjoy places!" I muttered as we lugged our bags over the tarmac and back to the plane.

We made our way up the East Coast without incident. I remember standing on the edge of the United States, mesmerized, as the white, frothing band of Niagara Falls roared over the edge and into the roiling abyss below. Mist floated high from the water's impact, so that it seemed to constantly drizzle rain, and we had to shout to hear one another speak over the falls' thunder.

Over the following ten days, we landed in Ohio, Michigan, Indiana, Illinois, and Wisconsin, flew up the west shores of the Mississippi River to Minneapolis, and on to North Dakota, South Dakota, and Hooper, Nebraska. From there, we flew to Rapid City, over the Black Hills of South Dakota. We had planned to go to Cleveland and Detroit too, but the Summer Riots of 1967 made the stops dangerous.

We stayed for a luxurious, two full days in Wyoming at the "Flying-A" dude ranch, situated against a tall mountain backdrop, surrounded by 600 acres of magnificent meadowland. Blue Penstemon, Lupine, Red Indian Paintbrush, wild white daisies, and yellow Alpine Wallflowers sprinkled the summer grass with color.

Mac, one of the ranch hands, drove us into the mountains over sage-brush and across riverbeds in a vintage 1945 Willys Jeep. My mother clung to the window frame of the windowless passenger door while Mike and I bounced around in the back seat. The more we yelped and whooped, the more Mac laughed. After a couple of hours we arrived at our 10,000-foot destination and set up camp. There were twelve of us, including the ranch hands and a family from New York who had ridden to the camp on horseback.

Mike and I explored the woods surrounding the camp while Mom regaled the other campers with stories about our adventures. Later, we ate hot dogs, corn, and potatoes cooked over the campfire, listened to Mac tell tales of the Old West, and sang camp songs until Mike fell asleep by the fire. Then Mom made us go to bed.

In what seemed like no time at all, a disembodied voice pulled me from my dreams. "Look, an elk!"

I rolled out of my sleeping bag and rushed to the tent flap, where Mike stood pointing. There, in the cold, pink mist of dawn, close enough to hit with a rock, stood an elk. It looked like a cross between a deer and a cow—as large as a cow, anyway—with great, spreading ant-lers. Mom came to stand behind me, and the three of us watched in in-timate silence. The elk eyed us placidly, then turned and lumbered away. I watched until it disappeared.

The following day we left the Flying-A behind, now just a dot on the map. The new-car-smell of the cockpit nauseated me after such grand wilderness, and I chafed at being in confined quarters again. I wanted to feel the ground beneath my feet and to stay in the same place for more than a couple of days. Our last stop would be Yellowstone National Park, where we would view Old Faithful and the Lower Falls. Then, we would head home.

Home. Whenever I thought of home, I thought of our house on Yew Street, before the divorce, before our family splintered. At the beginning of summer, I'd wanted to feel close to my mother and Mike, like we once had, and I supposed I did feel closer. But it wasn't the same. Everything was changing—the world, my family, me. Was I heading back to the same loneliness and confusion I'd left? Or would that change too?

I pressed my forehead against the cold window and watched as mountains and valleys, rivers and lakes, forests and deserts passed under the clouds beneath my feet.

JACKIE

For every hour learning to fly the plane, I spent three hours studying the books. I learned about weather, radio navigation, rules, and regulations. I read and studied and crammed for the FAA written exam until I thought I wouldn't remember a single fact.

On the day of my test, after what seemed like an eternity, the inspector looked me straight in the eye and said, "You need more practice on soft field and short field takeoffs and landings, a little more work under the hood, but I think you're safe enough to pass." He wrote "recommended" on my ticket. At that moment, I was sure if I flapped my arms, I would fly around the room.

For me, the most important part of the experience of traveling was the people I met. I loved the excitement of flying a machine, I enjoyed the cities with their architecture and buildings and culture, I loved the country with its changing geological structure, but most of all I loved the people—the men and women and children.

And people treated us as if we were special. Our kind of excitement was different from living each day in the secure, everyday existence of home, school, and work. But more importantly, it required a willingness to take risks. Liking people, being open and friendly, and trusting strangers provided us with valuable experiences: the man in Kansas who brought us to Marco Island; the family in Miami who took care of you and Mike; Whitney, the artist at Palm Beach who sketched us; the "big-wheels" who sponsored us at hotels and corporations all over the country; the family on that farm in Nebraska; Bill taking us all over New York; and Joe, taking us from Atlanta to D.C.

All these people supplied us with places to stay, meals, and interesting tours of their areas. In return, we brightened up their lives with conversation and excitement.

Still, I was anxious the whole time—not only about flying, but about Rick and John and life back home. It was hard for me to take as much freedom with my life as I did. I had to take you and Mike everywhere with me (and I liked doing that), and I would have taken Rick too, but he didn't want to go and didn't get along well with you two. So I left him behind.

And John, at Leavenworth. I'd worked so hard on trying to get him parole or clemency. It really was sad, the treatment they gave COs; it made me angry and bitter.

As we went back towards the West Coast, a part of me wanted to return home, but another part knew that when I got there nothing would be settled. I vacillated from worry to resentment because I had to pay rent for those three months for a house I wasn't living in, for the housekeeper, and for all the things I'd left behind—in addition to paying for the trip.

But problems are the challenges that take courage and strength required to battle. And the battle is what makes us know we're living, and alive, and feeling with all the joy and the excitement and the laughing.

So whenever I thought about going home, I'd laugh to myself. Where is home? What is home?

Sex Education

Bits of paper drifted through the air like snow, covering the flat bottom of the trash can. For a week, certain I was pregnant, I'd fantasized about what it would be like: cradling his (I knew it would be a him) tiny form in my arms; feeling his soft, warm skin against mine; inhaling his sweet, baby-powder scent; feeling the smooth, round curve of his cheeks with my lips. My boyfriend and I would have to get married, of course. He'd find a full-time job, and we'd rent a little apartment together. I'd be a good mother. Finishing high school would be the toughest part.

In 1969, if you were a pregnant, unmarried teenager, you went away somewhere until you had the baby and gave it up for adoption. The alternatives were grim. I'd heard about girls who tried to get rid of their babies using knitting needles or drugs, or went to "special clinics" in Mexico. I'd never give my baby up for adoption. I imagined how beautiful he would be, and what a wonderful life the three of us would have together. My boyfriend didn't know—I wanted to be certain, first—but I'd written my fantasies in my journal.

That morning, waking from a disturbing dream to the cool light of morning, I'd discovered blood in my panties. In an instant, everything changed. I felt light, free of the imagined weight of my baby. Still, my little family had seemed so possible, and so real, a vague disappointment loitered around the edges of my relief. I shook my head. How stupid.

Having a baby would be the worst thing that could happen to me. Everything I'd written was nonsense, I could see that now, and the evidence of my stupidity lay in pieces in the bottom of a metal can. For good measure, I threw a few balled up scraps of paper on top of the litter, grabbed my books, and went to school, shutting the door to my room.

When I came home that afternoon, the house was dark, the air unmoving and stale with faint smells of diapers and bleach. The blinds were shut, which wasn't unusual. Mom liked to keep light off the furniture, and my baby brother David was probably still napping. I blinked as my eyes adjusted. Mike and Richard were sitting on the couch in our tiny living room, looking bored and sheepish. Why was Richard here? He hardly ever came home, except when he was in trouble or needed a place to crash—but here he was, hands clasped between his legs. Why? And Mike—Mike, who never stopped moving, sitting still on a couch. Strange to see them hunched over like that, doing nothing at all—not even talking.

It struck me how much they looked alike with their broad noses and matching blond hair waving past their shoulders. Though they were six years apart (Richard was 18 and Mike 12), anyone would have known they were brothers. And something about them, their postures or expressions, transported me back in time, to junior high school days and our family encounter sessions. The muscles in my back and legs tensed—but we hadn't done sessions for a couple of years, at least. I eyed my brothers, suspicious. Mike fidgeted, tapping his heels against the front of the couch, looking expectant. So strange, all this silence. What was going on?

My mother, still in her teacher's uniform—a belted-at-the-waist knit dress and low-heeled pumps—walked into the living room from the shadows of the hall. At forty-eight, she was proud of her hourglass figure, the same size as when she was twenty, and she almost always wore clothing that accentuated her small waist. Mine had grown larger than hers somewhere around age eight. She faced me now, serious and anxious and tired-looking, as if she had waited hours for me to walk through the door. My heart lurched—someone must have had an accident and died or been hurt. Why was no one saying anything? She extended her arm toward me, her hand clutching a misshapen piece of paper. The page rattled like a snake as she shook it.

"What's this?" she demanded.

I set my books on a chair and walked closer to see what she had. There, taped together like a paper mosaic were the tattered bits of journal I'd discarded just that morning, each piece scotch-taped to the next, letters carefully matched to make words, sentences, paragraphs.

"What does this mean?" she asked. My mother's voice, like mine, was loud by nature—she was used to throwing it across a room of thirty-five high school students. It was like that now, but tight and controlled.

My mind, still seeing the shreds of paper as they fluttered from my hand into the trash, struggled to comprehend what she had done, and the time it must have taken to match the pieces to each other. I looked into her face. "You went through my *trash*? You had no *right* to do that!"

"Are you pregnant?" Her tone remained level, denying my right to outrage.

My eyes cut sideways to my brothers. Theirs didn't meet mine, but Mike wore that smirky, embarrassed, twisted smile of his. A hot, fight-or-flight panic pushed up through my throat and into the roots of my hair.

"No, I'm not. That's why I tore it up and threw it away," I said. "Why are you doing this to me? Why didn't you just ask me ... alone ... you know, *privately?*"

"You know I don't believe in keeping secrets," my mother answered. She waved the paper toward my brothers. "What do you think of your sister?" Neither one replied; it was a rhetorical question.

"You showed it to them? Oh my god, you had them *read* it?"

The room darkened further as tears stung my eyes. Just what I needed, to cry in front of my brothers, give them another reason to tease me. I rushed past my mother into my bedroom and banged the door shut.

"I *hate* you!" I shouted through the closed door, fell onto my bed, and sobbed into my pillow. Why couldn't I have a normal mother, one who cared how I felt? A mom who understood there are just some things you don't want your brothers to know. She was supposed to understand. We were supposed to be the same, she and I—allies in a family of boys. We used to be so close. Our hand-squeezing: one, two, three—I love you; one, two, three—I love you too. A lifetime ago.

You know I don't believe in secrets . . . yeah, right. Not those belonging to other people, anyway. I could hear their voices in the other room, not words, just tones: my mother, going on and on, my brothers' murmured low replies. Talking about me. I raised my head from my pillow. "Bull SHIT!" My heart beat hard, filling my ribcage. My lungs struggled for air. There was not enough air.

A black, blind rage flooded me, screamed through my pores. Desperate in my need, I looked around my bedroom for something to break, something that would hurt my mother. But there were only the nightstand with lamp and alarm clock, my trash can, a wood chair, my bed, and a brown painted dresser where my poor caged canary now chirped and jumped about on his perch, upset by the door slamming and the yelling.

I loved my bright yellow canary, how he woke me with trilling song every morning, and how, when I let him out to fly around my room, he would perch on the bleached cat's skull that sat on my windowsill. I loved my window too, a long, narrow slit of light high on the wall by my bed, because no curtains or blinds ever blocked its light. The canary and the window comforted me now, when I did not want to be comforted. I hated that I could never, ever stay angry long enough, hard enough. I willed myself to hold onto the rage, but failed.

That's what always happened: my rage faded, broke down, transformed, thickened. More Tar.

My mother didn't talk to me about sex, which even then I thought bitterly ironic since she had degrees in psychology and communication, facilitated those therapy groups for teens, and had taken in all those pregnant girls over the years. And I never understood why she could listen to and give guidance to others' children, but not to me or my brothers. Maybe it was because her students offered gratitude and adoration while we took her for granted, but I am guessing.

Mostly, what I learned about sex from my mother, I learned through what she did or said about herself. I learned it was possible to love more than one person at a time, as she had with the men I knew as my dad and my biological father; as she had with David's father and other men. I learned it was fun to flirt, exciting to feel desirable, and that a single woman had more freedom than a married woman. I learned you could find men to date through personal ads (that's how my mother met David's father and how I would, years later, meet my youngest son's father).

My mother told me, "Men are like children, and it's wiser to choose men who are not as smart as you. They're easier to control." I told her that was a callous way to approach relationships. "You'll see," she said.

For my thirteenth birthday she had given me—in front of my friends—a menstruation kit, consisting of a box of Kotex pads, an elastic sanitary belt, and a pink booklet titled *Becoming a Woman*. On several occasions (so I knew it must be important), she had counseled me to never date Catholic men because "they're screwed up sexually" and have a "Madonna-whore Complex," which she explained meant they could only be physically attracted to women they didn't love.

When she shared stories with me about the men she dated, her eyes shone like blue-sapphire jewels, radiating excitement. When she was pregnant with my youngest brother, David, she had asked if she should get married to his father. I said yes. Whenever she confided in me like that, I felt close to her, and I believed these were her ways of feeling close to me. Sometimes, in an ecstasy of closeness, a small secret of my own would gush from me in a fountain of trust. But such indiscretions on my part were always a mistake; what I told my mother became hers, and she believed in sharing her thoughts and feelings and views with everyone.

A week or so after our confrontation in the living room, my mother picked me up after school and drove me to Planned Parenthood. She parked the car under the shade of a large oak, reached into her purse, and pulled out a $20 bill. "Go in there and ask for some birth control pills."

"Aren't you coming with me?"

"No. I'll wait out here. Just go in and get the pills."

The girl behind the reception counter looked up as I entered the lobby. "Can I help you?" She was young, not much older than I was, and pretty, with long wavy hair.

"I'd like to get some birth control pills, please."

She handed me a clipboard and pen. "Fill out these forms, then wait over there." She pointed to four wooden armchairs lined up like bricks against the opposite wall.

"Can't I just get some pills?"

"The doctor has to examine you first, and we need to have your medical information on file." Her toothy smile flashed at me.

"Oh," I said, taking the forms, conscious of my mother waiting in the car and wondering how long this was going to take. I filled in my name and address and the date of my recent period, but didn't know the answers to most of the questions about family history or insurance. The girl said that was okay, to just fill out the forms as best I could. After I handed over the clipboard, I sat and looked around. The empty waiting area was small and austere, everything worn looking, but tidy, the walls painted the color of green cheese. Posters punctuated the walls—pictures of vibrant, smiling fathers and mothers with two children (always a boy and a girl), peach-skinned mothers cradling babies in their arms, and artfully photographed close-ups of rounded bellies backlit through sheer curtains. Beneath or above or around the beautiful pictures, slogans announced: *Planned Families Are Happy Families*, or *Plan, Prepare, and Protect Your Future*. Bold letters proclaiming *Planning Is Power: Use Contraception!* framed a teen couple pensively holding each other on a park bench. A low table piled high with puzzles, children's books, and toys filled one corner of the room, an island of primary colors in an otherwise olive-toned landscape.

After what seemed a long time, a woman in a white coat opened a door next to the reception desk. "Linda?" I got up and followed her into the examination room. She handed me a flat bundle. "Take off all your clothes, and put this gown on. The opening goes in front."

"All my clothes?"

"Yes, everything. You can leave your socks on, if you want." I looked down at my feet. "The doctor will be in, in a moment," she continued.

When she left, I took off my clothes and put on the paper "gown," which reached just below my waist. It was decorated with tiny blue flowers. Feeling exposed, I looked around and saw another flat bundle on the examination table. It turned out to be a large piece of folded blue paper, same as the gown, but flat. I wrapped the paper around me like a skirt and sat on the table, hoping the doctor would hurry up. Mom hated to wait. Why did they need me to take my clothes off?

After a perfunctory knock, the doctor entered the room, a tall, beefy mountain of a man with big hands and a big, round face. A million years old. Bald, with freckles on his scalp. The woman in the white coat slid in behind him and began pulling things from drawers. The doctor, brisk and business-like, towered over me where I sat on the edge of the table and asked why I was there. I repeated I wanted some birth control pills. Yes, I had a boyfriend, and yes, we were having sex. He frowned and turned his back to me, pushed his hands into skin-toned latex gloves the woman held ready.

"Lie back on the table, so I can examine your breasts," he said. I lay back, clutching shut the opening of the gown. He moved my hand aside and began feeling my breast, prodding, squeezing, making small circles with his fingers. I looked at the wall. "Arm up over your head," he directed. I complied. Did I know how to do a breast self-exam? I shook my head, and he placed a pamphlet on the counter. "Take this with you."

I sighed with relief when he was done and made to sit up. "Can I have my pills now?"

"Not yet." He extended two metal bars, terminating in what looked like metal cup holders, from the bottom of the table. "Lie back and put your feet in these," he instructed.

"What are you going to do?"

"A pelvic exam. Scoot all the way down to the bottom edge, put your feet in the stirrups, and try to relax."

Oh god, he's going to look at me, I thought. But I lay back and put my feet in the stirrups, pressing my knees together.

"Spread your knees apart. Further. Relax." The blue paper sheet obscured my view. The woman handed him a tube of something. Without a word, he slid his gloved fingers inside me. My knees pulled together. "Relax," he said again. He sounded exasperated. The woman came over and guided my knees apart.

"It won't be much longer," she said. Her eyes seemed kind, and I clung to them with mine.

The doctor felt around inside me while pushing down on the outside of my abdomen with his other hand. His fingers left me. "This might be a bit chilly," he said, as he inserted something hard and icy cold, stretching me wide.

I gasped and did my best to hold my trembling knees apart, but I could feel myself clenching. I looked at the ceiling and tried to breathe. Relax, relax, he's a doctor, he's a doctor, I repeated silently, but it didn't help. The woman handed him a Q-tip with a long wooden handle. Its sharpness surprised me as it delved inside. Then it was gone. I went slack as he slid the hard thing out and handed it to the woman to put in the tray of used items, where I could see it was made of stainless steel.

It's over, I thought, and started to relax, stifling another gasp when a burning sensation invaded my senses. It took me a second to realize the doctor had slid a finger into a place no one had ever touched before, a place I thought of as dirty, and was pushing it around. Shame burned through me.

"All done," he proclaimed. "You can sit up now." I pulled my legs together and sat up, wrapping the blue sheet over me, as if it would protect me from what he had already done. The doctor snapped off his gloves and threw them in the trash, scribbled something on a pad, and said, "Take one of these each day. Don't skip a day. And you need to take them for a full month before you can count on them to keep you from getting pregnant. Understood?" I nodded, my eyes level with his name tag.

He left. The woman in the white coat handed me the prescription and the pamphlet showing how to examine my breasts. She said, "You can get dressed now. Go to the front desk before you leave to get your first three months' pills and make a follow-up appointment." I waited for her to leave before I moved.

The pretty girl behind the desk handed me a small brown bag. I opened it. Inside were an instruction book and three round containers that looked like dials. "Remember to take one every day," she said. "That'll be $35 dollars."

I looked up, worried. "I only have $20."

She frowned, then sighed. "Well, we'll take what you have." Relieved, I handed over the $20 bill my mother had given me and walked on rubber legs to the car. I slid into the passenger seat, clutching the paper bag on my lap, and handed my mother the prescription.

She said, "What took so long? I have things to do!"

"The doctor had to examine me first." I looked at the floor. I wanted her to ask about what had happened, to say something comforting. I wanted to ask if a doctor had ever done that to her, but I didn't know how.

"Where's the $20?"

I looked at her in surprise. "I used it to pay for the pills."

"Damn it! Why did you do that?"

A low buzzing began in my ears, and my vision swam with black dots. There wasn't enough air. "Th...they wanted $35, but they said they would take what I had," I tried to explain. "I had the twenty."

My mother's voice filled the space between us. "We could have gotten them for one dollar at Kaiser!" as if I were stupid and had no sense, as if I should have known.

I began to tremble again and then to cry. "Why didn't you take me to Kaiser? Why did you give me $20 if you didn't want me to spend it?" We were screaming at each other.

"Because I didn't want anyone to see me! I didn't want anyone to know that my fourteen-year-old daughter needed birth control pills!"

My mouth, which had been open, ready to spew venom, snapped shut. Now it made sense. This—the going in alone, the exam, the doctor's unspoken contempt, the woman in the white coat's pity—was what happens to shamed girls, and the mothers who were ashamed of them. I turned away and leaned my wet cheek against the cool glass of the passenger window.

My mother backed the car out from under the tree. We rode home in silence.

I never talked to my mother about sex. I didn't tell her about the time Bill had taken her, Mike, and me up to Lake Berryessa and we stayed in the same motel room; I had awakened to whispering, had watched the moonlit silhouette of her nightgown as she slid it from her body, and I had pulled the covers over my ears so I didn't have to listen. I never told her about the year I was eight when one of my relatives would sneak into my bedroom at night with his jar of Vaseline, roll me on my stomach, and rub his prepubescent penis between my fat thighs; he didn't hurt or penetrate me, but it made me feel wrong, and I'd been unable to defend myself from his soft coercions, his whispered *Pleases*, his persistent assurances. I hadn't told her about the man whose ride I accepted from school one day who took me into the woods, forced my lips open with his tongue, and then abandoned me to find my way home after I began crying. I knew I'd been lucky.

Nor had I told her about that first painful and disappointing time, when I was thirteen. I'd been curious, and the boy—a sixteen-year-old high school sophomore—was insistent. I knew he had a reputation for "loving and leaving," but my curiosity won out, and I said yes. I hadn't even started my period yet.

I couldn't talk about these things with my mother—not because she would be angry or didn't believe in talking about sex, like most parents, but because I was certain of one of two responses: denial, or telling everyone within earshot what I had done. These were my stories, not hers to tell. It hurt me that she didn't understand the difference, and it meant I couldn't confide in her or ask her for guidance.

My mother and I never talked about that day with the journal, or the day we went to Planned Parenthood. And, until now, I haven't known how she would describe those incidents. Sifting through a stack of letters, I find one to my brother Terry.

"This 'poem' was thrown away in my kitchen," she wrote, telling him she had "accidentally" stumbled upon my journal page while checking to make sure I hadn't tossed out important homework. She didn't tell him that she'd searched my bedroom trash, or that she'd taped the bits together, or that she had used Richard and Mike in her confrontation with me.

Her lies crash over me like a wave of ice water. For a fraction of a second, I question my sanity: Did I *invent* tearing up that journal page and throwing it in my bedroom trash? But then, in a stack of letters, I find the taped-together journal entry, fragile from age.

I have been searching her letters for pieces of myself, for her accounts of our shared experiences, because a part of me has believed that I'd find a truth more reliable than my memory. Or, at least, an adult perspective. I feel stupid. But then I remind myself of my true purpose—to discover who my mother really was, to understand my anger, and find a way to reconcile with her. In this case, my anger was justified: she understood what she did was wrong, and had lied about it.

I never believed my mother to be cruel—only insensitive. I knew she loved me, but I was her child and to her way of thinking children's feelings were nothing more than passing storms.

She wrote:

I can't identify with Linda. But, I love her for all the things I'm not: a fantasy child, unrealistic, undisciplined, and irresponsible. We can't be around each other for a whole day. I work too fast, too efficiently, too organized, too disciplined, too everything, and the poor child falls apart around me. She's a dreamy, unrealistic kid who had visions of being a mother. ... So she learned how I would react and how she felt too, all without paying the price.

She was wrong about what I learned, but she was right about some things: I *was* dreamy and unrealistic and silly.

My mind shifts to my own children, how often I told them they were unrealistic or undisciplined. When my daughter was fourteen, she thought she would become a star by walking the streets of Rodeo Drive. She insisted that if I would *just* take her there, a famous director—or better, a famous actor—would "discover" her and lift her to the fame she deserved. I told her that her dreams were unrealistic. When he was thirteen and fourteen, my youngest son and I battled over his "right" to stay out all night. He claimed he would be happier sleeping on park benches and eating out of garbage cans than living with my unreasonable restrictions.

As for me, it seems that I remember who I wanted to be, not who I was.

In that letter to Terry, my mother reproduced some of what I'd written in my journal. I'd forgotten that I'd gone through a confused, religious phase, somehow believing in reincarnation and God and Jesus and meditation and multiple universes and ghosts all at the same time. Or that I'd written to myself as if the voice of God were speaking to me about it being "his child" within me, to trust in Him, and so on. I don't remember myself that way. I remember myself as spiritual, imaginative, wild, full of life, intelligent, purposeful, and disciplined. But I think now these are constructs of my adult mind. I was, after all, a normal teenager, biting at the ropes holding me to childhood, no matter how fragile or necessary.

My mother believed her actions would open windows of understanding to the world. Instead, I learned to bury deeper into myself, to hide or burn things I didn't want others to read, and to never trust my mother with information close to my heart. I learned how to be alone.

At fourteen, I could never have imagined that, thirty-two years later, I would take my own sixteen-year-old daughter to Planned Parenthood for birth control pills. The scenario would be much the same. Except, she and I would have talked about boys and the joys, dangers, and responsibilities of sex. I would give her a play-by-play description of the entire exam process before we went, would sit with her in the waiting room, would request a female gynecologist, and would stand by the exam table holding her hand saying, "It's all right, Sweetie. It's just something all women have to do." And I would never, ever stop worrying that I hadn't listened enough, explained enough, comforted enough, or kept her from feeling that shame.

Did my mother worry about how I felt or whether she had been there enough for me?

If we could discuss it now, what would my mother and I say to each other? I suspect that even now, she would say, "You were my Cloud Nine girl."

JACKIE

My life was like the swinging of the pendulum—lifestyles constantly switching back and forth—always at my own bidding but, nonetheless, the changes were difficult. I went into marriage and motherhood at a young age, then left being a housewife to become a professional woman, then left marriage to become single. About the time I adjusted to and loved being professional and single, I switched back—at age 46—to being married and, for the first time in 12 years, the mother of a new baby. Then in less than a year, I swung back to being single again. In one life that's a lot of switching back and forth. I made the choices, but the emotional price was high.

The year you turned fourteen, we moved twice, and I was single, pregnant, married, and divorced—but glad about having your little brother, David. It had been a big decision. I'd talked it over with you kids and with David's father, but only I could take responsibility for the decision and answer for the results. I had a few momentary conflicts about the responsibility and lack of freedom—but the balance was 95% on the joy-grateful-to-be-pregnant excitement of a new life.

After David was born, and after the divorce, and after his father moved out, I sometimes felt that I had lost myself through him. I was no one. Nobody. I didn't have a job, I didn't have anyone to talk to or relate to, I was alone and lonely, I didn't know what to do or where to turn.

At the same time, you and I went through such a bad time. You were growing and changing—a beautiful girl. I loved you terribly, but we were at the divorcing stage. I was trying to let you go, let you be independent, and I thought I was doing a pretty good job of it. I told you I would find you another place to live anytime you felt we were fighting too much, but you said you didn't want to go, and I thought we could stay friends and still get through the transition.

I could let my teenagers go—I sent John away when he was fifteen and a half—but I thought you and I might have been able to work it out. We had such special feelings for each other and, since you weren't a boy, I couldn't swamp you as easily.

But I intensely disliked the girls and boys you were going with, so unintelligent and immature, with no future. Why does a little girl want to experience grownup living? I felt sorry for you, your turmoil. Yet I believed you had to find your own way out of it.

I saw in you and me a pattern I lived with my own mother. It was a destructive pattern that took me many years to get over—if I did get over it. I saw my own mother as "the wicked witch," the bad, punishing, cruel person who set up all the restrictions, rules, and limits to my freedom. I never heard one kind word, or recognized one generous deed. Not because she didn't say or do them, but because I selected not to hear or see them. I needed the fallacy of my mother as the guilty one to blame for all our differences. I saw my mother as a selfish, neurotic, sick person who cared only for herself.

You were stronger than I was and fighting for your freedom and rights as an individual. You seemed to be experiencing too much of life too early and at times your hands shook, as if you couldn't handle it. I wondered if I was supposed to be a strong parent for you. But I wasn't strong, and I couldn't set strong limits. Sometimes I thought you were asking me to set them, and I tried. But in a fight you were stronger than I—and you knew it. So, in the end you got your way.

On My Own

I can't remember what day of the week it was, or whether there was any run up to the conversation. But I remember the way the dusky, late afternoon light filtered through the drapes in our living room, accentuating the drab, beige furnishings—as though the world had been washed of color, leaving my mother and me facing each other in an old-fashioned, brown-tinted reality. It was six months before I would graduate from high school.

"I found a place for you," she said.

"What do you mean?" I asked. My mouth tasted acid, like new metal fillings.

"I've arranged for you to live with a couple nearby. You'll get room and board in exchange for cleaning house and helping them with their new baby."

I went still, but my mind raced. We'd been fighting for months—a lot, and about the same things. She said I was selfish and lazy; I said she cared only about herself. She pushed; I pushed back. I shouted; she shouted. I slammed doors and pouted; she slapped me and pulled my hair. We'd been insufferable, but I hadn't *really* meant it, all those times I told her I hated her and didn't want to live with her anymore. Well, yes, I had meant it, and she'd told me she placed an ad in the paper, but I never thought she'd actually make me leave. I hadn't thought anyone would take me. I hadn't really thought about it at all.

I wasn't yet sixteen.

I looked down, not sure what to say, not sure how to feel. I couldn't really blame her if she wanted to be free of me. I was pretty sure she didn't know how much LSD I'd been dropping, or about the speed I kept hidden in the pages of my dictionary, under "S." So it wasn't that. I was always home by my 11:00 curfew, so it wasn't that either. No, it was because I kept telling her I was old enough to make my own decisions. I kept telling her to leave me alone. Now I'd gotten what I wanted, what I'd asked for. Right?

"I think you'll like them," my mother said encouragingly. "They're young and seem nice, and you'll only be a few blocks away. It's ideal. I told them you were very responsible."

Me? Responsible? I didn't know how to clean anything except the dishes. Mom had always complained that I didn't do a good enough job, but she never had the patience to show me what she wanted. She said it was easier to do all the cleaning herself.

Now, she looked at me expectantly, and I could see she thought she was doing me a favor, thought I would be pleased.

I turned up the corners of my mouth, trying to appear happy. But my gut had twisted into a knot and my feet were rooted in place. I felt light-headed, as though I were standing on a high bridge, the wind whipping my hair—jump or fall, the result would be the same. Terry, John, and Rick had all been out of the house by ages fifteen or sixteen. Now it was my turn. Why should I be any different?

"I've arranged for you to meet them after school tomorrow."

"Um. Okay," I managed, and snuck a look at her face. Did she look disappointed?

I knew I shouldn't have been surprised, yet I was. I couldn't object, couldn't tell her it wouldn't work or that I was too young, couldn't say: "I'm only fifteen. I need to be home longer. I need someone to show me how to live and how to take care of myself."

Thinking about it now, I see us as part of a long line of mothers and daughters always at odds, always failing at their attempts to find common ground. My mother and I, my mother and her mother, her mother and the mother before her. Eventually, my daughter and I. What would it take to break this chain?

I've known mothers and daughters who seemed close, who had relationships of mutual trust and respect. But as a teenager and later, as a mother with a teenage daughter of my own, I have come to view those relationships as unreal—mythical, magical sleights of hand, smoke and mirrors—concealing the true conflict that lies beneath the surface, hidden from view.

I moved the following week. As I packed my clothes and books, I saw how little actually belonged to me: three or four boxes of clothes, a box of books, my guitar, and my canary—my beautiful, yellow, singing canary. Mike was helping carry my stuff out to the car, the birdcage in one hand and a bag in the other. In the driveway, he stopped to adjust his load and moved the birdcage to his right hand. His palm pushed up into the false bottom, tipping the cage. It fell to the ground, upside down and bottomless. Frightened, the little bird flew into a nearby tree and then away, a flash of lemon disappearing into the trees. I shrieked.

More than once, his song had kept me from slumping into lonely depression. Now he was gone, and I didn't have hope for his survival—there were so many cats.

Mike looked at the birdcage on the ground, and bit his lower lip. His empty hand hung limp by his side.

The young couple lived in a small three-bedroom bungalow with a tiny front yard and an even smaller backyard. Bryan was handsome, with olive skin, strong features, and dark, wavy hair that fell just short of his shoulders. Susan was petite, with cropped, ash-blonde hair, tiny upturned nose, and a pregnant belly that ballooned impossibly large in front of her, their baby due any day. That evening, Bryan and Susan and I sat in the living room sharing a joint in celebration of my arrival (Susan wasn't smoking because of the baby). I marveled at my luck to be living with such cool people. Everything would be okay, after all.

Six weeks later, Susan fired me. I was more trouble than I was worth, she said. I left hair all over the bathroom and messes in the kitchen. I didn't know how to clean and didn't do anything unless I was asked. It was all true. I cried and begged to be allowed to stay. I would do better, I promised. But Susan said I was just too young. I knew she was right, and I blamed my mother for not teaching me how to clean, for not preparing me for life, for throwing me into this situation. The blame, added to all the hurts and confusions and angers of the past, was too painful to acknowledge, so I pushed it deep inside where it smoldered.

My boyfriend Paul and I moved into a one-bedroom apartment next to the freeway, in a complex of old, one-story, brown-shingled buildings surrounded by tall redwoods. But for the roar of traffic, the grounds, covered as they were with years of redwood needles and detritus, could have been mistaken for a rustic retreat center on the California coast.

Paul, an eighteen-year-old artist I'd met at high school, wasn't particularly good looking; he was short, pudgy, and pale-skinned, with limp, shoulder-length blond hair so thin you could see through to the pink of his scalp. But he created fine, carved-wood jewelry, clay sculptures, and blown-glass pieces, and his artist's sensibility—his intensity and dark, brooding nature—intrigued me. Beneath his surface angst I saw a sensitive, creative being. But when my mother met him, she said he and his family were "beneath" me, to which I replied that she was a hypocrite and that our family had its own share of alcoholics, welfare scammers, and jailbirds, and how was our family any better than his?

Neither Paul nor I had a job, and I don't remember how we managed to scrape together enough money for a month's rent. We had no furniture, only a mattress, a couple of saucepans, two sleeping bags, pillows, boxes of clothing, and our guitars. Somehow, we made a ten-pound bag of potatoes—all we had to eat—last several weeks.

In our third week in the apartment, I caught a whiff of something burning and went into the living room to investigate. A dark cloud of smoke billowed past the front window. When I cautiously peered outside, I could see it was coming from our neighbor's apartment. I pounded on his door, but there was no response. I ran from apartment to apartment pounding on doors, until I found someone with a phone. By the time the firefighters arrived, the blaze, fed by the dry shingles and layers of redwood needles, had erupted through the roof and was eating through the kitchen wall into our apartment. And by the time they extinguished the fire, we didn't have an apartment to go back to.

We borrowed money from friends and moved into a remodeled garage studio, but we weren't there for long. Without steady income, Paul and I moved from place to place: from studio apartment to basement, from rooms with friends to a bed on the floor of a trailer, and—for a brief time—to my mother's cabin in La Honda, which we shared with three of my brothers and a string of hippie friends. I picked up temporary work waitressing and telemarketing. Paul picked up occasional jobs. But it wasn't enough, never enough, and it seemed we were always at the receiving end of someone's generosity.

Through it all, I clung to the belief that I had to finish high school and, six weeks after I turned sixteen, I officially graduated. Since no one in my family would attend and there seemed no point in participating in the ceremony, I walked into the school office to pick up my diploma. As I walked out and down the long path leading to the street, a vague sense of loss jostled with my sense of accomplishment. I wondered what I would do next.

So when a pharmaceutical company hired me as a machine operator, I felt I'd hit the lottery. I suddenly had a full-time job with good pay and benefits. We could afford rent and food and a car. But after two years, Paul grew tired of me. He started mocking me, calling me stupid and shallow, saying that blondes were more attractive and he was going to leave me. I would cry and beg him to stay, swearing I'd try harder and be everything he wanted me to be.

The worst part was that I believed him: I believed I was stupid and shallow and ugly, and inwardly I shrank into myself, becoming smaller each day, until the day something snapped. On that day, when he said, yet again, that he would leave me, I told him I was tired of his constant threats and that if he wasn't going to leave, I would. I grabbed a handful of clothes, walked out the door, and went home to my mother, who seemed immensely pleased to have Paul out of my life.

By then, she'd bought a huge duplex on Embarcadero Road in Palo Alto and had begun a cooperative living experiment with a group of people. I moved into one of the unfinished rooms in the third-floor garret, where I cried myself to sleep every night for six weeks. And when I was done crying, I quit my job and went to community college.

I met Eric at my friend Mary's birthday party, a week after my eighteenth birthday in April of 1973. I had seen him once before in front of the piano practice rooms at Foothill College, where we both studied music. He had appeared suddenly, an apparition in his floppy leather hat and wild shoulder-length hair, his fierce blue eyes intensely absorbing me. A white macramé bag hung from his left shoulder at hip level. His unusually long arms terminated in expressive, long-fingered hands that gesticulated as he spoke. I can't remember what he said. I only remember feeling dazed when he disappeared, as though I'd been hit by a sleeper wave at the beach.

The party was held at Mary's parents' house, a large ranch style home on a hilltop in Los Altos, California, with spectacular views of the Bay Area and sloping lawns surrounded by oak and eucalyptus trees. There were about fifty of us, mostly music students from the college. A small group of us stood in a tight circle around Eric, passing joints and laughing.

"There'll be two choirs, piano, and a small orchestra. Harp, too. But the voices will be the primary instruments," Eric said, illustrating the rise and fall of imagined melodies with wide sweeps of his arms and articulate fingers.

"How are you going to get the choir teacher's approval?" asked Charlie, a boy with long and already thinning, dirty blond hair. I thought he looked like a young Benjamin Franklin, minus the glasses.

"Oh, pfff," Eric said, waving his hand in quick dismissal. "Once he hears what I have in mind, how could he turn it down?"

"Thank you, darlin'," he said, reaching out to receive a joint from the girl next to him. He put it between his lips, and inhaled deeply.

Eric's charismatic flamboyance attracted me. I edged nearer, lingering, wanting to know more. When his intense eyes focused on me, it was as if everything and everyone else faded away. When I remember it now, I picture us centered in a halo of brilliant light, surrounded by nothing but shadows and silence. If we had been in a movie, they would have used a circling camera to give the impression that we were twirling slowly together, locked in an eternal moment.

Giggling like children, the two of us snuck outside and around to the front of the house. We peered through the picture window into the living room as if through a window at the zoo, and made fun of the primates inside. We played hide-and-seek in the dark among the leafy shrubs. We danced under the stars to imaginary music.

When we walked back into the living room to rejoin the party, I was breathless with excitement. I had never met anyone with such concentrated energy, anyone so unconcerned about how he appeared to others and so ready to engage the imagination. But then, Eric flopped his lanky body down onto the couch next to Mary and draped one arm around her shoulders in comfortable intimacy.

How could this be? How could I not have known? What should I do? I retreated and watched them from a safe distance on the other side of the room, my gut a turbulence of confusion. When Mary went to the bathroom, I followed her into the hallway.

"Mary, can I talk to you for a minute?" I had no idea what I was going to say.

She stopped and turned to face me with raised eyebrows.

"I think I'm in love with your boyfriend," I blurted, only realizing the words were true as I said them. "I didn't know he was your boyfriend," I rushed to explain. "I would never have let this happen had I known. What should I do?" If she told me to keep my hands off him, I would let him go.

Instead, she looked at me curiously and shrugged. "He's his own person. Do what you want."

After that, I spent as much time with Eric as possible, following him around, dreamy eyed as a groupie, entranced by his flair for the dramatic. A self-taught piano player with a chord-pounding style mix somewhere between Elton John and George Winston, he was in the process of inventing the double choir piece he'd talked about so passionately that night of the party. I say "inventing," because he didn't actually write it. First, he sold the teachers on the idea. Then he talked several musically talented people, including Mary (a flute player like me), Dirge (a cello player), and Charlie (keyboardist and bass player), into transcribing his musical ideas. I'm not even sure Eric was enrolled at the college.

Eric had a remarkable ability to get people to do what he wanted. Imagine: a guy who can't read music, looks like a hippie, and walks like Liberace, waltzes into a junior college and talks several teachers, the college administration, and sixty students into performing an as yet unfinished piece, and *they* do the transcription.

When we hitchhiked together, instead of putting out his thumb and waiting for someone to pull over, he would scrutinize the cars and drivers as they approached. When he selected the ride he wanted, he would point his index finger at the car, make eye contact with the driver, and then point to where he wanted the driver to pull over. Nine times out of ten, it worked. I had nothing but admiration for his manipulation skills. (Nineteen years later, during post-divorce therapy, my counselor would tell me that I'd married a male version of my mother, and I'd be astounded by recognition.)

During the transcription sessions, Eric played chords on the piano, hummed parts of melodies, and gave directions while waving his hands in the air as though weaving invisible webs of enchantment. Charlie dictated the orchestration. Mary and Dirge hand inked the arrangements. I watched.

On weekends, we partied at the apartment Eric shared with his mother (who was rarely home), smoking pot and hashish and skinny-dipping in the apartment pool at midnight.

Eric had six girlfriends, including Mary and me, all musicians. I didn't care. It had been only a few months since I'd broken up with Paul, and I didn't want anything from Eric but his attention. In fact, I felt sheltered by the emotional buffer the other girls provided. But, one by one, they slipped away like sharks smelling fresher meat elsewhere, leaving him to Mary and me. I didn't notice their absence.

When I stayed at Eric's, he'd sleep in, but I would get up and go to school. If I left my books at my mother's house in Palo Alto, I got up extra early so I could retrieve them and still get to school on time.

"Why do you have to get up so damned early?" he'd complain as I rolled out of the twin bed we shared.

I shrugged. "Because I have to. I don't know why, but I have to go to school. It's important to me." Eric would groan, flap his hands at me to say goodbye, and then turn over and pull the covers over his head.

One Saturday afternoon, Eric and I sat cross-legged facing each other on a small Indian rug in the living room of his apartment, smoking hashish, when someone knocked at the door. It was Mary. She stormed in, glancing briefly in my direction.

"We need to talk," she said to Eric. "In private."

They walked into the bedroom and shut the door. I felt unattached; whatever she was upset about didn't concern me. After only a minute, Mary swept out of the apartment without saying goodbye.

"What happened?" I asked.

"She gave me an ultimatum," he said. "Told me I had to choose between you and her."

"What?" I waited for him to give me the bad news. Of course he would choose Mary. Who wouldn't? She was talented, sexy, earthy, a better flute player, way more desirable than I. Was I about to be thrown out?

"I told her, if I had to choose, then it was you," he said.

On the night of the concert, Foothill College's auditorium was packed. The singers filed onto risers on each side of the stage, and we musicians took our positions on chairs below them. A gleaming black Steinway filled the center. The curtains rose and Eric swept onto the stage in a black, embroidered silk, kimono-style robe to audience applause, everyone's attention riveted on him. He bowed, sat at the piano bench, raised those long-fingered hands in the air, and descended on the piano with the energy and earnestness of a lover.

The choirs were brilliant. The cellist played with longing. The flutes and woodwinds sang like birds. As I played, I focused on Eric. His long, wavy hair flowed behind him as his head bobbed up and down with the music, his tongue bitten between his lips in an endearing form of concentration.

As the final notes hung in the air, the audience jumped up, cheering, clapping, whistling, and stomping feet. Eric stood and bowed, gesturing grandly with open arms at the choir and musicians on stage with him. This moment of splendor would not be his last, but it would be his finest. Never again would the world give him such adulation. But that night, he was high on life, on music, on being the center of attention. And I, on him.

We were married that New Year's Eve, just eight months after we met, in a nondenominational ceremony at a church three blocks from my mother's house. The bridesmaids, who had all made their own renaissance-fashioned dresses, and the groom's men, who wore whatever they wanted (Charley wore a black cape with red silk lining over a tux), walked in pairs down the side aisles. As each couple arrived at the front of the church, they took their places on the stage, picked up their instruments, and began to play. Each new pair added layers of melody and rhythm, until there were four flutes, a harpsichord, a cello, an organ, a string bass, an oboe, and a harp. Eric waited for me at the altar dressed in a midnight blue, embroidered velvet robe we'd purchased in Berkeley, looking exactly like a blond, sandaled Jesus in commercial East-Indian garb. His ankles stuck out plainly below the hem of his too-short robe.

I wore a dress of shimmering, winter-white crushed velvet that my maid of honor, Mary (yes, the same Mary) had made for me. It had a princess waist and long, bell-shaped sleeves. On the bodice front, Eric's grandmother had embroidered a sunrise in vibrant colors. A slim braid curved from the crown of my head to the back of my long, straight hair, joined by a solitary marigold. I clutched a colorful bouquet of blossoms in both hands, and a nervous rash of small, rosy pimples adorned my face.

The bridesmaids and groomsmen began our wedding song, written by Eric. My father, whom I hardly ever saw since my parents' divorce ten years before, but whom I loved and still wanted to please, took my arm and walked me down the center aisle. He placed my hand in Eric's and then took his seat between my mother and stepmother.

I'd never seen my mother so dressed up. She wore a baby blue ankle-length chiffon dress with a white lace bodice that had long sleeves ending in lacy ruffles. A blue satin belt accentuated her waist, and pearls circled her neck. She'd had her hair professionally colored and set (usually, she colored it herself at the kitchen sink with whatever five-and-dime auburn hair dye was on sale). And she wore makeup: pink lipstick and false eyelashes. As I took Eric's hand, she dabbed at her eyes with a handkerchief.

I took a deep breath to calm my trembling hands.

The minister began in the usual way, "Dearly beloved, we are gathered here..." then veered into a mishmash of romantic wedding fantasies that Eric and I had devised for him. Symbolizing the union of our spirits, we each took a lit candle from our attendants and together lit the large candle centered on the altar. Symbolizing the union of our souls, we drank wine from the same cup. We knelt before the altar where crowns of wildflowers were placed on our heads. We promised more than we could ever be to each other.

"I promise to be always by your side in sickness and in health, in joy and in sorrow, through good times and bad; to love and cherish you beyond death and for all eternity," Eric said, as he slid my silver and turquoise ring onto the third finger of my left hand.

"I promise to be always by your side in sickness and in health, in joy and in sorrow, through good times and bad; to love and cherish you beyond death and for all eternity. Wherever you go, I will go, and wherever you lodge, I will lodge. Your people shall be my people, and your God, my God." I had no idea that this last part, a line Eric wanted to include, was from the Book of Ruth in the Bible. It was true—I would follow him anywhere—so I thought, why not?

We were pronounced "Husband and Wife." We kissed. We turned. The minister introduced us as Mr. and Mrs. Eric Peterson. Eric opened his arms wide to our audience and intoned, "Let the party begin!"

JACKIE

Most kids have to hate their mother to divorce themselves from her, and I went through it with each of my kids. But I felt like a scapegoat, a product of twisted reality. Everyone blames the mother. Even you said, "You're just too strong."

I knew for years that you (and Terry and John) couldn't bear to listen to my voice. What were the choices? Not to talk? Not to say anything much at all? To small talk and never get at anything real? Hell, I just had to be me. You kids didn't know me. You only heard and saw "monster mother." It was hard, and I cried a good deal. All I could do was turn it off, say to myself, "Such is life."

I was a great one for kicking my kids out early. It seemed to me that we avoided a lot of the pain and cutting up that parents and teenagers do to each other. I loved you all, but knew I couldn't live with you without being destructive, so the best solution seemed to get you safely away where you could be yourselves.

So, the summer of 1970, when you went to Europe with your high school group, I started thinking about wanting to move closer to work. I planned to start my PhD program in the fall—only two night classes per week—but life would be full. I thought I'd rent a room with David, or we'd get room and board someplace, Mike would go live with his father or with John at the cabin in La Honda, and I'd find a place for you. I wrote and told you I was going to put an ad in the paper: "Senior girl wants room and board in exchange for babysitting." I thought you could stay with me every other weekend.

I looked forward to not having all the work of keeping a house, shopping, cooking, and being responsible for so many people all the time. I'd keep the front part of the duplex, so if it didn't work out you could quit and come back home.

After you moved in with Paul I worried about you, not hearing from you or knowing where you were most of the time. If being a "good" parent is to raise kids that are independent, free souls who can go off into the world on their own, then apparently I was a successful parent. You didn't seem to need any kind of contact at all. I wanted to know how you were, what Paul was doing, whether you were working, what you were thinking and feeling.

I worried about you on many levels. Being a teen is a terrible time in life. It seemed to me that you were searching for a father figure, and Jack was never able to be that for you. You weren't really a "Carr." None of us held that on a conscious level, but I knew it was a big deal for you underneath everything. You would talk about your real dad, wonder where he was, have fantasies about meeting him. It seemed to me that you didn't know who you were or what was real. And you couldn't talk to me—never were able to talk to me—maybe because I wanted so desperately to have you share yourself with me. I knew you wanted to—you tried—but you just couldn't.

Then, after you and Mike were gone, I was restless and needed to do something. So I found the twenty-room house on Embarcadero in Palo Alto. It was ideal—close to work and to Stanford—for the extended family kind of living I wanted to do. I imagined filling the place up with "grandparents," teens, students, singles with children. I could see us holding hands, having evening encounter sessions before the immense fireplace. Teens living up in the attic. I would set it up as a corporation with everyone involved and invested. Many people were finding the little single-unit, close-knit family stifling, incomplete, boring, dull, and restrictive. It took special people to function in an extended family situation, but in California there were hundreds of really turned-on, neat people ready and willing to explore new kinds of relationships. It was exciting.

I felt so relieved when you returned home and decided to go back to school.

When you and Eric came to me and said you had something you wanted to tell me, my first thought was that you were pregnant, and then that you wanted to borrow some money. So when you said you wanted to get married, I was stunned. Eric did most of the talking, do you remember? God, I couldn't believe how he went on and on, fantasizing about your relationship—how perfect it was, how you'd been made for each other and were destined to meet.

As he described the wedding ceremony, I imagined it would be like the production he put on at Foothill: Eric up front and center directing a fantasia with colored strobe lights and choirs and strings and flutes. I could even hear the applause from the audience, and see Eric in his Guru costume shaking his long hair up and down.

When I offered you $2,000 to elope (an exorbitant amount!) or $1,000 to pay for a wedding, you chose the wedding. I have to admit, I kind of liked that, though I was afraid you wanted it more for Eric than yourself. You were both glowing, enclosed in a rosy pink bubble with the world shut out. I knew that you'd just turn off any advice I had to give, so though I saw hard times ahead, I shut my mouth and gave you what support I could muster.

How could I say what I really thought—that Eric was a leech, a hypocrite, self-deceptive and no damned good? You loved the guy and you needed to believe in him. The very fact that he asked you for money for his piano and for his truck (so he could "work"), the very fact that he always expected people to do things for him and to pay his way indicated a serious character flaw. In truth, he frightened me.

But I felt you needed to trust and believe and then get hurt. Otherwise you'd never know. You didn't want to look at it, and I didn't want to rub your nose in what you already were trying hard not to look at.

When you left, you said, "I love you ," and I thought, what else is there?

That Old-Time Religion

Three days after the wedding, Eric and I loaded everything we owned into our sky-blue Chevrolet Suburban and headed north along the California coast to Vancouver, Canada. It was 1974, the winter of gas shortages, long lines, and steep prices, and we were driving into the coldest January either of us could remember. The temperature on the coast had plummeted, ocean winds pulling more frigid air from the north. Frozen tendrils of water hung from plants, and thick icicles clung to the steep cliffs along Highway 1.

Eric had outfitted the pickup bed of the Suburban with two, narrow, top-loading plywood bins, one on each side. Into these we had piled clothing, toiletries, camping cutlery, and dishes. Between the bins we slid a mattress, sleeping bags, two plaid wool blankets, and pillows. Though we had little money or food, we had a case of wine and a pound of pot left over from the reception, and an extraordinarily rosy view of the future. We stowed the pot in one of the bins. The box of wine functioned as my footstool while I rode shotgun.

Our strategy was to drive until we ran out of gas. Then I would stand next to the truck, gas can in hand, and wait for a Good Samaritan to stop—one always did. He (our Samaritan) would take us to the nearest station and give us a couple of dollars for gas. If he seemed cool, we'd offer him a joint. Sometimes he'd give us a few extra bucks for food and water, or we'd trade an ounce of pot for cash. At the station, we'd wait in line, fill the can, hitchhike back to the car, and drive until we ran out of gas again. If we didn't make it to a state beach or parking lot, we'd spend the night on the side of the road.

It took us over two weeks to reach the Columbia River Gorge. Multnomah Falls, normally a roaring rush of water cascading from a height of over 600 feet, was frozen solid except for a fine, persistent stream spraying over the top. We posed for pictures on the bridge beneath the falls—me, imagining myself a French tourist in my crocheted beret and scarf, and Eric, grinning and standing on one leg, both hands turned upward in a "what can I say?" gesture. We crossed to the Washington side of the river and found an isolated turnout in which to park for a few days. The spot commanded a picturesque view of the icy, churning river, with the falls as backdrop.

During the day, we'd explore the river trails and trek the surrounding hillsides, but the cold would drive us back to the shelter of the truck before long. The wind was so strong that one day, climbing on the nearby rocks, I experimentally relaxed my weight against the gale's force—and did not fall. Biting winds slapped the Suburban around at night, making it difficult to sleep. And we were not near bathroom facilities; when I had to pee, I was forced to bare my tender skin to the subfreezing wind and then wait, trembling, until need overcame discomfort. I envied Eric his ability to unzip and let go from the comfort of his clothing.

Young and crazy-in-love, everything the other did was perfect. Holed up in the back of our truck, we got stoned and made love and talked for hours. Eric painted broad strokes of our future where we would play music, be surrounded by talented, creative people, and live off the land. I spoke about gardening, the perfection of living for art and music, and the pure nature of the human spirit.

One night, we dropped acid—probably not the wisest thing to do, seeing how the two of us were trapped by the darkness and wind in a four-foot by eight-foot space with only our unwashed bodies, a pile of wool blankets, and each other for company. Just as I began experiencing small shifts in my reality—colors becoming more vibrant, shapes becoming fluid—Eric opened one of the wooden bins, dug elbow deep into it, and produced a small, white leather book.

He waved the book in his hand. "It says here, 'The wages of sin is death.'" He paused. "But 'the gift'—the GIFT—'of God is eternal life in Jesus Christ.' Eternal life! Do you understand? *Really* understand? It means *this*," he patted his chest, "*this* body, *this* flesh, will be resurrected and made immortal because of Jesus' sacrifice."

I stared at him, dumbfounded. Knocked so off center I could barely register what was happening. How could I not have known he owned a Bible? We had packed those bins together, and I was sure I knew everything in them. I had been sure I knew *him*. Yet Eric, with the flourish of a magician pulling a rabbit out of his hat, had pulled that Bible out of *our* bin. We'd been apart for three months prior to our wedding, and I knew he'd made new friends in Portland while I finished the fall quarter at Humboldt State, but that couldn't explain this stranger before me. Could it? And why now?

"By believing in the Son of God, Jesus Christ, we will be saved from sin and from decay and corruption." Eric's voice—the singing voice I loved—rose and fell in the age-old cadence of the circuit preacher, arms and hands conducting his symphony of words. He looked the part, too, with his wavy, shoulder length hair and earnest, bearded face. Only his glasses were out of place, his blue eyes boring into me.

I must have gawked, mouth open, eyes shifting between my wild-eyed husband and the white leather book in his hand. "What are you saying?" I finally stammered.

Here's the thing," he said, "it's all based on *faith*. You only have to BELIEVE to be resurrected."

The wind outside roared and shook the Suburban. His voice faded to the background as I retreated into my mind so I could think about what was happening. Who *was* this man? We were married—had both said "I do" for better or worse. Married! I had promised him, "Wherever you go, I will follow; your people will be my people, and your God my God." I hadn't taken that last part seriously; it had been a sweet, romantic gesture. I didn't even know Eric *had* a God.

Though I'd been raised without religion, I'd attended Catholic services with a friend in grammar school and Baptist youth groups in my early teens. I'd always felt there was *something* larger out there, some thinking, conscious entity that guided the world. Why not Jesus? Could I make a decision to believe so deliberately? So logically?

What would I do?

I saw my future then like a road stretching before me in a long line to the horizon. Only minutes before, Eric and I had been walking that road together, hand-in-hand. Now the earth beneath our feet was shaking, the ground fracturing between us, a thin crack dividing the road into halves, he on one side, me on the other. And though I sat within the shell of our truck, surrounded by wool blankets, warm and protected from the wind, I shivered.

Eric had stopped talking and was watching me. I looked up into his eyes, which now seemed flecked with steel. "Will you come with me into Paradise?" he asked, and stretched out his hand as if inviting me to dance.

I hesitated.

Whatever effect the LSD was beginning to have had vanished in a rush of cold clarity. With this decision, I had the power to make or undo us. If I said no, the crack would widen until it became a crevice and then a chasm, until we no longer could hold onto each other. If that happened, our marriage would be over, and I would lose him. What would I do without Eric?

If I said yes ... well, what did that mean? It meant taking my wedding promise literally: his God would be my God. It meant making a decision to believe the things he was saying. It meant letting go of doubt.

I took a deep breath. I jumped over the crevice.

We never made it to Canada. Instead, we drove the Suburban south over the Columbia River to Portland and parked at the curb outside Paul's house—he was one of Eric's new friends—a singer, guitarist, and fundamentalist Christian. There, I met Barney, another musician and key influence in Eric's (and now my) conversion from agnostic to born-again believer. That Sunday, we joined their congregation, a group of about twenty-five people who gathered in their pastor's mobile home for three-hour Sunday services and mid-week Bible study.

A haze of cigarette smoke enveloped us as we entered the single-wide home. Men and women and children crowded the pastor's narrow living room, and it seemed as though every adult except Eric and me were smoking. I didn't know what to make of the scene, it was so unlike any church I'd ever known. Women, cigarette in one hand, puffed contentedly while pressing their nursing babies (modestly covered by blankets) to their breasts with the other. I had quit smoking just before our wedding, and the acrid tang of cigarette smoke, once so comforting, now made my throat close and eyes water.

I smiled and ducked my head as Paul introduced us to the pastor, a hard-edged man of about forty. He also had a cigarette in hand. "Have a seat, we're just about to begin."

A couple of the mothers took the older children into a bedroom for Sunday School. Then, Paul and Barney played guitar while the congregation raised their hands in the air, sang hymns, and intoned in a language I didn't understand.

I must have looked confused, because one of the women leaned toward me and whispered, "They're praying in tongues. It's God's gift bestowed on believers by the Holy Spirit."

"Oh, thanks," I whispered back, having no idea what she meant.

After the singing and praying, the pastor delivered his sermon through tendrils of tobacco smoke, shouting about Faith and Absolute Righteousness and pounding his fists. People cried and shook, clapped their hands, and shouted "Hallelujah!" and "Amen!"

We went to church services every Sunday and Tuesday. I learned from the other women what it was to be a good Christian wife: subservient, supportive, hard-working, modest, gentle, quiet, and prayerful. Our role was to take care of our husbands, children, and home. The man was the head of the household, to be respected and obeyed at all times. The women were warm and generous, bonded by a shared belief in a greater calling. They helped one another in times of need, and they welcomed me into their extended family.

It wasn't long before a core group of us—musicians with a mission of bringing the world to Jesus—took over a five-bedroom house and set up a commune in Portland. We called ourselves "The Beulah Land Band." And, from 1 Corinthians 9:14 ("... the Lord has commanded that those who preach the gospel should receive their living from the gospel") we believed God would provide for our needs. After all, weren't we doing His work?

God's provision took the form of visiting local missions and charities, such as Loaves and Fishes, for handouts of donated food. His provision took the form of hocking my grandmother's wedding rings—the ones my mother had given me after my wedding—to feed Paul's two hungry children. It took the form of church members paying our rent and utilities. God's provision always came in one way or another, and though sometimes we had nothing to eat but a fried paste of flour and water, we thanked Him mightily for His generosity.

We believed we were special, but the Beulah Land Band was part of the cultural wave of communal living and Jesus Freaks and bands that crashed over American shores in the late '60s and early '70s. Like those other groups, ours—along with wives, children, and hangers on—quickly outgrew our living space. We rented a thirteen-bedroom nursing home in Lincoln City, on Oregon's rugged coast. Situated just off Highway 1, the front door of the dilapidated, green stucco building opened onto a beach parking lot. Tall blackberry-covered sand dunes sheltered one side of the long building from coastal winds; a grass field bordered the other side and wrapped around the back. The rental agreement included a small two-bedroom clapboard cottage sitting on the back part of the property. All for a ridiculously low monthly sum.

Jobs were hard to come by in Oregon, even harder on the coast, but across the street and a block toward the highway stood a Mo's Restaurant, famous for their clam chowder and peanut butter cream pies. I managed to get a part-time waitressing job there. Eric weaseled his way into a wine sommelier position at the Inn at Otter Crest, a ritzy resort restaurant about five miles south. He didn't know the first thing about wine, but he had enough showmanship and nerve to fool most people, including the restaurant manager. A couple of the men found odd jobs from time to time, but most didn't work. And, since our living arrangement required everyone to put 100 percent of earnings into the communal pot, no one had much incentive to search. At the height of our population, there were thirty of us: five married couples, four children, two single women, and fourteen bachelors. Only five of us worked, part-time, at or below minimum wage. Two of those five were Eric and I.

The men would lounge in the large front room strumming guitar, talking, and smoking cigarettes. The women cleaned house, cooked, tended to the children, and bickered over the fair distribution of chores. I worked six days a week. On the seventh, I spent the entire day in the kitchen, starting before dawn baking the eight loaves of homemade bread we consumed each day, and ending after the dinner dishes were washed and put away.

Though we women were subservient to our husbands, everyone was secondary to Paul, who never worked a day during the year we lived there. He was prone to periods of depression when he would refuse to emerge from his darkened room for weeks at a time. I remember his wife, Joan, bringing meals to him in bed, their two young boys tiptoeing around to avoid their father's wrath. But Paul was a creative, musical genius. He had a magnificent tenor voice with more than a four-octave range; he played guitar, bass, and pretty much any other instrument he decided to learn; he was our musical inspiration, the head of the band, the one who always had final say on policy decisions, and our default spiritual leader.

Without Paul, there would have been no Beulah Land Band. His vision for reaching out and spreading the Word of God through music was the glue that kept us living and working together, in spite of disagreements among our members. Paul, Barney, and Eric formed the musical core.

Throughout the summer, we gave community concerts on the lawn behind the home and played for open-air weddings. As the days shortened and the weather chilled, we learned new songs, including cover tunes with moral messages, and played in local clubs. Our tips gave us enough to get by for another day on our diet of whole wheat bread, rice and beans and, when we could afford it, cheese.

As the fall of 1974 stretched into the winter of 1975, tourists stopped coming, resorts and clubs closed down for the season, jobs were lost, and new ones impossible to find. Savage storms heaved giant logs crashing against the steep cliffs and through the lower story windows of high-priced hotels. The wind whipped rain in stinging staccato against anything in its path. Reasonable people shut themselves in their houses with their wood stoves and waited for the winter to pass.

But I, a lone, dark figure, hunched forward against the wind, could be seen haunting the beaches of Lincoln City during those tempests. Weighted down and bulked up by fisherman's waders, layers of sweaters, a heavy coat, and a plastic, hooded poncho, I trudged the sandy length of the beach gathering the treasures that washed ashore during such storms: sand-polished blue agates; blood red and emerald green jasper; petrified burl from redwood and myrtle trees, their minerals gleaming in swirls of rich reds and browns; and the rare, whole sand dollar.

The force of the wind was so strong that as I lifted each foot the wind pushed me backwards, and I could see the indentation of my foot— before instead of behind me—already filling with rain. Unable to hear anything but the pounding waves and roar of the screaming gale and exhilarated by the wildness of it all, I yelled wordlessly into the wind. I could shout and scream and holler, and no one would hear me—my voice blowing back and away too quickly even for me to register. I relished having the beach to myself. It was the only place I could be alone. The only place I could raise my voice without social retribution.

After that dark winter, in late spring, my mother came to visit for the first time since we'd moved to Portland. Ten months earlier, an antique glass doorknob had shattered in her hand, the shards cutting deeply through the nerves and tendons of her palm and fingers. She'd had reconstructive surgery, followed by months of physical therapy, but it ached all the time and she was unable to fully open her hand or lay it flat on a table. The pain made it impossible to do many of the activities she enjoyed, like knitting and typing, for any extended period of time.

We led my mother toward a folding chair in the center of the living room, where she perched on the edge of the seat as though ready to bolt. Knowing this was all strange to her, I couldn't blame her for being jumpy. Through the window the midday light, diffused and bleached by fog, illuminated her in a soft, dreamlike lambency. Though she was over fifty, her skin appeared smooth, unwrinkled except for the deep worry lines between her brows. She sat still and quiet—like a small animal caught in a trap. Trapped by the need to be polite. I felt a little sorry for her. So when she sat back, lowered her head, and placed her hands in her lap, I found myself wishing things were different. That I hadn't pushed upon her my—our—desire for her to understand God's healing power.

Her right hand—the injured one—trembled, whether from trepidation or nerve damage, I didn't know, and she covered it with her left. We believed God miraculously healed the sick and that He would heal her. And we believed that healing was our right as born-again-Christians, if only we had enough faith. But questions of faith pestered me. Didn't the person being healed have to have faith too? Could our faith be substituted for her lack, and would it be sufficient? If faith is unquestioning, do questions indicate a lack of faith? Did the very fact that I had questions short-circuit the possibility of healing? If so, how could I keep doubt from creeping into my mind?

Faith, I told myself, is believing in things unseen, being certain of the uncertain. We were trusting faith to perform a miracle, transforming not only my mother's hand, but her heart as well. I couldn't admit to doubts; to admit having them would be to give them power. It was better to deny doubt, to assert my faith over it, erase it.

Six of us circled around her, joined hands, and began praying and speaking in tongues.

As the leader—the Elder—of our group, Paul began: "Oh Lord, we bow our heads and come before you in humility. We ask you to fill us with your presence and the power of your Spirit. We beseech you to touch Jackie with your Spirit that her hand might be healed, that *she* might be healed and be made whole, saved by the power of the one true God: the Father, the Son, and the Holy Spirit."

"Amen," we responded. "Praise the Lord!"

My mother had bowed her head with us and was staring at her hands, clasped tightly on her lap.

Paul produced a small bottle of holy oil from his pocket and poured a drop onto the crown of my mother's head, and then he took some on his thumb and anointed her forehead with it. She closed her eyes as he did so, and I wondered what she was thinking. Was she feeling the power of prayer? The presence of God? Paul laid his right palm on her head and raised his left hand high as we crowded around, putting our hands on her slim shoulders and back and arms.

Eric's voice boomed over our heads, "We call on the power of JESUS, and demonstrate to all the angels of Heaven and Hell the POWER of our Lord Jesus Christ to heal the sick and bring the dead back from the grave."

"Amen!" we chorused.

"Ah-la-ca-rish-te-endo-si-ba-ra-ka-ya; ca-na-la-shee-tay; ca-na-la-shee-tay."

The rest of us joined in, singing and praying in tongues, weeping and crying out, eyes closed, voices raised in a cacophonous crescendo, until we were spent all at once and fell silent.

"In the name of the Father, the Son, and the Holy Spirit, I proclaim you HEALED!" Paul said, punctuating the fact with a small, final, shove, pushing my mother's forehead upright and backward.

She opened her eyes and looked down at her hand, which lay on her lap as bent and broken as it was when she entered the room. Thin white scars still crisscrossed her palm, their violence fracturing the lines that, if whole, might have foretold her future. Her embarrassed eyes met mine, and I saw at once that she was not embarrassed for herself, but for me.

After I had made my decision that night in the back of our Suburban to follow Eric into Christianity, I experienced only a brief period of intellectual resistance before embracing what I was told to be the Truth. Religion became the frame upon which I hung all my hopes for a better life—better than what I thought my mother offered. King James Bible-speak became my new dialect and, in addition to saving the world, I began the effort of saving my sinful mother. By letter.

Going through her boxes, I find these letters mixed among other correspondence. Reading them now, I see that the very letters I had been *sure* communicated the love of God amounted to nothing less than an attack on her values and lifestyle. I try to excuse myself: I was blinded by youth, just eighteen and nineteen when I wrote these letters; I lived in a judgmental, religious bubble, and I didn't have enough self-awareness to understand the thick, ugly, anger within me.

I cajoled:

> I pray for you constantly, that God would soften your heart and turn it towards Him. For that is where real and absolute love comes from. Why do you think Eric and I are so happy? We are bound in unity by the love of God. Simple. I wish to have a similar relationship with you.

I preached:

> Do you trust your riches, or the government, or medicine, or scientists, or the work of your own hands? They are all false, because they are not led by God. "Do not lay up for yourselves treasures on earth … but lay up for yourselves treasures in Heaven, where neither moth nor rust consumes and where thieves do not break in and steal. For where your treasure is, there will your heart be also." Matthew 6:19-21.

I criticized, believing that the only way she and I could have a "real" relationship would be if she admitted her failures and believed in God as I did:

> I truly wish to be your friend and to love you, but I find it difficult to pass through your wall—your concept of self: Jackie Carr, the teacher and exciting woman who has allegedly done everything! You speak of family love. I have never seen or felt

such a love. There is no love or warmth or genuine fellowship in our family—only a cool distance. You call that respect. My brothers only use you. They bear no fruit because they have no roots. They are indecisive, deceitful, and selfish.

In attempting to save my mother—and she, being faithful to relay everything I said and wrote to the rest of the family—I managed to alienate my brothers for years to come. My mother, to her credit, did not give up on me, but kept trying to explain her point of view.

It hurts to view myself as she must have seen me: spoiled, sanctimonious, critical, unthankful, and arrogant. I don't want to admit I wrote these letters. I imagine my daughter writing like this to me and I cringe. I don't want to admit that I was ever this awful.

JACKIE

*I had my own dreams and my own experiment with communal living—
without the religious trip. Of course, you weren't paying attention to what
was important to me. By January of '75, my "big house" on Embarcadero in
Palo Alto had nine adults, three children, and Mike, and we used both sides
of the house—20 rooms plus the attic. It was working beautifully at first, and
gaining a reputation in the Santa Clara Valley area as an "alternative
lifestyle." People were constantly stopping by to see the place. Mostly, they
struck me as dreamers. Fantasy people who wanted to enjoy community
living vicariously, without any risk.*

*Then I bought the place and became everybody's "landlord." As soon as
that happened, people began to direct a great deal of hostility and
resentment towards me—leftover stuff from their pasts with mothers,
teachers, and authority figures. Saying things like, "Don't tell me what to
do," and "You look down on us."*

*The wounds and pains of that time stayed with me. Just thinking about
it brings a lump to my throat. Misunderstood, sad, emotionally battered,
and deserted, I told myself their hostility wasn't personal. I had more
financial and emotional investment in the cooperative living concept. I had a
higher level of commitment than they did. Why should I have expected
theirs to be the same as mine? The problems really began with my own
unrealistic hopes and expectations. As always, the distance between the
dream and the reality was too great.*

*What I really wanted—was starving for—was affection and love. But all
around me, I found only emotionally bankrupt people, unable to truly love
or be loved, looking only for "fun" and surface emotions that wouldn't cost
too much. Men everywhere, emotionally and financially bankrupt; others
recuperating from broken relationships with no energy to give; others
married and "stuck" in a horror I wanted no part of. I have never wanted to
be involved in the lives of people who don't know when to scuttle their*

sinking ships. I had to get away from them, while still wanting the attention, affection, and love they could give.

I was like a pendulum, swinging back and forth between intimacy and freedom. Confused, re-evaluating, re-assessing my responses all the time. The suffering was terrible. The ache of it set my stomach quivering, my nerves on fire. To know that the despair would go away didn't help. I wanted to put the pain in a sack and drown it, dissolve it, but it wouldn't go away.

You didn't know that I had someone in my life I really cared for, someone I thought I might want to live with, even marry. But after ten years of creative-single-living, I just couldn't go back. The price was too high: the terrible boredom, the taking each other for granted, the feeling caged, as if I didn't have the right to be anywhere or with anyone I wanted; the having to answer to someone 24 hours a day, 7 days a week, 365 days a year.

In the end, I had to take what each relationship had to offer, for whatever length of time it existed. That had its price, too, but the price wasn't as high for me as the alternative.

Then you started sending me all those letters full of everything you thought was wrong with my life. Yes, I deliberately chose to stay on the surface with you. I didn't want to get into "your trip." I didn't mind your getting into it. But when you tried to sell it to me ... God <u>damn</u> it! ... there is no One Way for everybody, no Truth for everybody. If there was, then why has Christianity spent 2,000 years spreading "The Word" and "The Truth" and it hasn't taken?

Look, I wanted you to have "your thing" if that's what you were choosing, but not to sell it to me. Religious bigots turn everyone off because they aren't at peace with what they believe. I told you then that if you continued to run around trying to convert other people, you would only turn them away from God.

I always loved my life: my education and my job, my security and my freedom, my flying and my travels, my children and my men, my relationships, what I was into with some of my students, and what I meant to other people (not to my children, but to others). I didn't need to defend myself or justify my life to you. I had choices about what to do with my life. You didn't. You had no education, no job, no money that would have allowed you to choose, so you were stuck with what you had. You chose that.

In the end, your religion and your marriage weren't enough for you, either, and you moved on. Like me, with Jack, you had a good marriage with Eric—until you didn't, and the pain of staying grew to be more intense than the pain of leaving. Like me, you did what you had to do.

In the end, I knew you loved me, and you knew that I loved you. There were many barriers that divided us, but none so high that time and love could not break through. That was my faith and my religion and it gave me moments of joy and happiness, along with pain and separation.

From Mother
to Grandmother

"**P**ush." She spoke with quiet urgency.

I lifted my head from the pillow. "Now? But I'm not having a contraction."

"Yes, now."

I looked at my midwife and then at Eric, hovering over her shoulder at the foot of the bed. He seemed serious but not alarmed. Pokerfaced, both of them. I shrugged and bore down. My baby slid, slippery and wet, into the midwife's hands. I waited to hear whether it was a boy or a girl, waited for the baby to be placed in my open arms. But the midwife was busy doing something at my feet. I could hear sucking noises. No infant wailing. Eric hovered, eyebrows scrunched together.

"What is it?" I asked. "Is everything okay? Why isn't the baby crying?"

"It's a boy," said Margie, without moving her attention from the baby. "Just a moment. He needs suctioning, then I'll give him to you."

"A boy? Are you sure?" I'd been so certain I would have a girl, a tiny, pink layette lay waiting on the changing table next to the bed. I hadn't even bought any boy's clothing.

The midwife smiled at me. "I'm sure." A moment later, she placed my new son's tiny form in my arms, cord still attached. He lay there, a blue frog, jerking in silent hiccups but not breathing.

"Why is he so blue?"

"The cord was knotted and wrapped around his neck," she said. "But he'll be okay." Eric wrung his hands, said nothing.

The baby's tiny mouth opened and shut, opened and shut, like a fish. "Breathe, baby, breathe. Please breathe," I whispered. There was no sound. Ten, twenty, thirty, forty infinite seconds. I massaged his chest, his cheeks. Tears sprang to my eyes. "Oh God, please let him breathe!"

Then he pulled air into his lungs—a loud, long drawing in of life— and with the exhale came a scream, as if outraged about having been pushed into this cold, bright place. My fear let up as the baby yelled, his blue face purpling with indignation, but he cried for forty-five long minutes, and there was no comforting him.

Margie recorded the time: 5:12 p.m. on May 12th, 1978. At that very minute, a plane with my mother aboard touched down at Portland International Airport. Though I'd called her that morning and told her I thought I was in labor, I didn't know she'd arrive so soon. Later, I would consider this auspicious, this numerological coincidence of my second son, Evan, and my mother landing on Earth at the same moment—5:12 on 5/12—but then, I was too busy trying to figure out how to comfort my newborn child.

I have always hated how movies portray labor: a woman clutches her abdomen in sudden agony, mouth open in surprise, and is rushed to the hospital where she screams for hours as though she's being murdered, swearing and growling at everyone around her; or the amniotic sack breaks, dumping what must be five gallons of water in public, rendering the poor woman helpless and incapable of thought. Labor is nothing like that. It sneaks up quietly, after months of mild, preparatory contractions known as Braxton Hicks, named after the man who first described them.

Braxton Hicks contractions can be difficult to distinguish from early labor. But that morning, around 10:30 or 11:00, I knew immediately. Felt that intense, cramping sensation deep inside, near the floor of my pelvis, more focused than usual. So I stripped the bed, lay down plastic sheeting, started a load of laundry, and cleaned house, "helped" by my twenty-two-month-old toddler. I told him, "You're going to be a big brother!"

Ezra had also been born at home, and his birth had taken twenty-six hours of regular contractions and four hours of relentless, hard labor, followed by an hour and a half of pushing. That experience told me this would be a long day, so I waited until mid-afternoon to phone my midwife.

"How far apart?" she asked, of the contractions.

"Oh, about twenty minutes," I guessed. I had also left a message for Eric, at work: "No need to rush home. Call later to check in."

Margie—a plump, competent, and practical midwife—arrived with her three children in tow to see how I was doing. Her oldest daughter looked after Ezra and the younger kids while Margie and I retreated to the bedroom for my examination. The phone on the nightstand rang, and I picked it up. It was Eric. "Oh, I think it'll be hours yet," I said.

Margie interrupted, "You better tell him to get home. You're seven centimeters dilated."

The next half hour was like a Keystone Cops' comedy. Bumbling about between my contractions, we made desperate phone calls to find someone to come get all the children, got the bedroom ready, brought in Margie's birthing equipment, prepared hot water, and laid out receiving cloths.

Evan arrived forty-two minutes after I had hung up the phone with Eric, and after only thirty minutes of hard labor and six pushes. Eric barely made it home in time.

After the Beulah Land Band and the commune disintegrated from a combination of acrimony and poverty, Eric and I and another couple from church rented a house in Portland. That's where my first son, Ezra, was born.

When I was eight months pregnant with my second, we moved into a white, two-bedroom trailer perched on five acres in Brush Prairie, Washington, an hour northeast of Portland. Mostly open pasture, the ground sloped gently down to a wooded area where a year-round creek sliced the land. An A-frame, corrugated metal-roofed barn was the only permanent structure. We had purchased the land with money my mother gave me—cash equivalent to the La Honda property shares she gave my brothers. It was our first real property, and the first time we lived alone as a family. We had grand plans for our chunk of land, dreaming of someday building a house and raising our own food.

The single-wide trailer, made livable by a push-out expansion wall in the living room, had also been provided by my mother—a loan we would pay back at $125 a month.

Brush Prairie couldn't properly be called a town or even a community; it was a post office and a general store, about a mile up the road from us. We were five miles from the nearest large grocery store, but still within commuting distance from Portland where Eric had gotten a job working for a landscaping company. After work, he often played piano in our friend Tad's band, and could be away from home for up to twelve hours a day. With only one car, Ezra and I had been pretty much confined to the trailer during that last month of pregnancy—except for Sundays, when the three of us spent the day at Crossroads Four-Square Church, the newest of what I would later come to think of as "big box churches."

So that last month of pregnancy had been a challenging and lonely time for me. Following Adelle Davis's recommendations from her book, *Let's Eat Right to Keep Fit*, I'd consumed a quart of her orange-juice-raw-egg-brewers-yeast concoction every day. The baby and I were healthy, but I'd gained sixty-five pounds. I had just enough energy to take care of my active toddler and the house, and to try to keep a little space around our home clear of the two-foot tall grass invading the rest of the pasture.

We'd had little choice but to let the grass grow. Some Saturdays, Eric would climb up on our tractor—an old, rusted red vehicle that belched clouds of black smoke and for which we didn't yet own any attachments—pull Ezra up on his lap and drive around the lumpy grounds, our toddler yelping with joy. On dry days, I would pack a picnic, and the three of us would forge a path down to the creek, where we could search for crawdads and—the ultimate activity for little boys—throw rocks into the running water, seeing who could make the biggest *kerplunk*.

Ezra had been two weeks late. I couldn't bear the thought of carrying this baby for so long and on my due date drank mineral oil diluted in orange juice to initiate labor—a home remedy my mother swore by, saying it had worked for her every time. All I got for my efforts was a miserable twenty-four hours of severe intestinal cramping and false labor.

I resigned myself to my fate, and though my mother had made plans to fly up on the baby's due date, I asked her to wait until after the birth. I should have known she'd catch the first flight after learning I was in labor. When it came to babies and childbirth, she had a habit of surprising me.

We didn't have medical insurance, and the cost of having a baby in the hospital was more than $1,200—far beyond our means. So I decided to have my babies at home attended by midwives. In spite of the fact that home births were illegal in Oregon in the '70s, they had become fairly commonplace, especially in the religious community. All we had to do was claim it had happened by accident.

I thought my mother would be upset about my deciding against going to the hospital, so every time she asked where I was having the baby, I avoided answering.

"Why do you keep changing the subject every time I ask where you're having the baby?" she finally asked.

"I've decided to have the baby at home with a midwife." I held my breath, waiting for a burst of criticism.

Instead, she laughed. "Is that all? My grandmother had twelve children at home. It's what women have always done." I relaxed then.

My mother loved babies; they transformed her into an earlier version of herself, a woman who dreamed of being a better mother than hers had been. And she always longed to be a grandmother like the ones she'd had, a grandmother you could go to when you needed solace your parents couldn't provide. A grandmother like the ones I hadn't had.

No longer simply mother and daughter playing our old tug-of-war power games, we were mothers, joined to each other and to all the generations before us by an infant's helpless cries—women, helping and learning from each other. My children had transformed our relationship, at least some of the time.

Now, I looked forward to her visit.

In spite of weighing in at a little over nine pounds, Evan was long and scrawny and wrinkled. He looked like a miniature old man, with inch-long blond hair that had a habit of standing straight up from his head like a cartoon character with his finger stuck in an electric socket. Evan wouldn't stay skinny or cartoonish for long, though. At two weeks, he weighed sixteen pounds, and the first time I brought him to church, I found myself arguing with a woman who didn't believe he was my newborn; he was too large, she said, and kept looking around as if I'd hidden my real child elsewhere.

But in his first week, Evan developed colic and cried more than eight hours a day. I'd lost blood and needed to rest. If it weren't for my mother charging into our little trailer with all the energy of a school teacher, bustling about cleaning and cooking and keeping Ezra occupied, I'm not sure what I would have done. All my church friends lived in Portland

and had their own families to take care of. And Eric was hopeless around children. I would never be able to leave them alone with him, because he'd get involved in a project and leave them unsupervised. A fact that didn't escape my mother.

We were in the living room, enjoying a rare moment of quiet. Ezra, who was having a terrible time adjusting to a little brother and had been acting out, was finally napping. Evan nursed as I held his warm little body close and rocked the chair, my toes playing with the gold shag rug. My mother sat in the other swivel chair, folding diapers. She looked disheveled and tired; none of us had slept well. "Have you thought more about my offer?" she said.

I shook my head. "It's not going to work out."

"I want you to offer Tad ten thousand dollars to buy the 2 1/2 acres between your land and the main road. Your land'll be worth more. Then you can sell it and move back to California. Right now, there are some good deals on land—with houses on them."

"Mom, we've been over this. First of all, Tad doesn't want to sell. Second, this is where Eric works, where our church is, where all our friends are. Besides," I added, "I don't want to owe you more money than we already do." Since my mother believed to owe money was a character flaw, I hoped that last point would carry weight.

"Well, what are you going to do out here all by yourself after I leave? Eric's useless. He's gone long hours, can't handle the kids, can't do anything but his music." She spat the word *music,* as if it was something distasteful. I knew she was right. I could feel the heat rise into my cheeks. Sure, I needed help now, right after the birth, but when I healed I'd be fine.

"I can take care of myself," I said, stroking Evan's hair. He was asleep now, his breathing gentle against my skin. I adjusted my blouse, moved him to my shoulder, and began patting his back. "Let's talk about something else, okay?"

"You need to get Eric to put in that drainage ditch. Otherwise, when the rains come you'll be in trouble. Didn't you have money left over after closing?"

"Yeah, we did, but we needed to pay some bills."

"Until you learn to live on less than you earn, you'll never get ahead. I've always lived on less than I earned."

I sighed.

"I'm just trying to tell you what works."

Here we go, I thought. She's like a tape recorder stuck in an endless playback loop. "The only person we owe money to is you," I said. "If you don't want me to be in debt, *stop* offering us money. And can we please talk about something else? About the babies, the weather, anything?"

"I hate small talk. You know that." Her eyes narrowed. "And let's not get caught up in pride and control issues. I'm simply suggesting you make some wise decisions and take action now instead of this prolonged drifting and dreaming. I'm not saying I think buying these five acres was a mistake, but I don't think it's going to work for your future."

"What do you mean?"

"Well, if you don't want to sell it, maybe you should deed back the property so I can hold it in trust for you. Just until Eric gets some kind of training. A trade. A profession. *Something.* The government has a lot of programs for young people who aren't earning enough—like Richard, getting that government grant to go back to school. Unless he gets some training, Eric will go on working for $5 an hour and never be able to support a family."

"Mom, we're doing okay. Let us be."

"I'm just saying. With two kids, you need *one* person in the family with a future profession. Clerks in supermarkets make $12 an hour in the Bay Area. And I don't like it that you're so far away."

"I know, Mom." I wanted to be sympathetic, but I liked the physical distance between us. The idea of having to interact with my mother on a daily basis distressed me. Someday, Eric would do something more than manual labor. Someday, I'd go back to school. I knew that. But for now, why couldn't she just let me be a housewife, enjoy my babies, and grow a garden? If she wasn't nagging me about something, she wanted to go on and on about my brothers and their problems. One or more of them was always in jail or in financial trouble or fighting with her about something, and it never ended.

Evan's weight pressed warm and heavy onto my chest. "I need to lie down," I said, pushed myself, wincing, out of the chair and lumbered down the hall to my bed, where I lay down with Evan tucked in one arm.

Ten minutes later, Ezra's high-pitched toddler's voice roused me. I heard my mother's footsteps on the carpet and her whispering to him to be quiet because Mommy was sleeping.

I *am* grateful for your help, I thought. I just want to live my own life.

JACKIE

After you wrote to tell me you were pregnant with your first baby, I thought of you every day. I kept hoping you'd come back to California to have your baby. When the boys had babies, I always felt they belonged to their wives' families. But you were mine. I had this fantasy—did I ever tell you?—about you having twins: one for you, and one for me. I love babies. They feel so warm and good. But then they grow up and become brats.

I wanted my grandchildren to grow up knowing me. I wanted to be the kind of grandmother mine was. My mother was depressed and stayed in bed all the time, constantly scolding me for making noise and telling me I was a "bad girl." And when she did, I'd run to Grandma, and she'd make some lemonade and put me on her lap and say, "Everything comes out in the wash." But when you took the money I gave you and bought the land in Brush Prairie, I felt cheated. And I thought, Okay, if my grandchildren are not going to be around, not going to grow up near me, then I should put all my love and energy into some other young ones who are geographically close. But I didn't know who that would be. So I just felt cheated.

I wanted you to be happy and financially secure, but you wouldn't take my advice. You wanted to dream. I don't think I ever told you that Jack and I bought five acres with my mother and dad and my sister when we were all young, when the boys got back from the war. We had big plans for a family community—three houses—and got so far as to go out on Sundays with our picnic lunches and build a magnificent, huge, brick barbecue. Then eventually, we were lucky enough to sell the land for what we paid for it.

You had the same kinds of dreams. And you were lucky too. Your land value appreciated so much that you could sell it a year later for twice what you paid and buy a house closer to town.

You believed I didn't understand the stages you were going through, but I did, because I went through them too: those early years with babies, nursing, wanting to get ahead. Jack was an apprentice mechanic. I took in laundry, babysat, boarded children, rented rooms—did things you would find "horrifying" to earn a little money.

After I returned from visiting you, John laid into me, telling me everything he didn't like about me: He said everyone was tired of hearing about my book, my work, my boyfriends, my problems around the house. I used people, he said. I talked too much, was too critical, and didn't have any friends because all I cared about was myself, and boyfriends couldn't hang around because I didn't know how to have "real" relationships. He said that none of you needed my help. You didn't need your teeth fixed or your rent paid or your cars fixed or anything, and that you'd all get along fine without me.

The problem was that when I helped, I put all of you in a position of feeling obligated and indebted. So when I needed help, like the lawn mowed or the driveway swept, none of you wanted to do it, and then you felt guilty.

Times like that made being a mother more pain than joy. I could stand it when all of you had problems, but I couldn't stand it when I got that barrage of negative judgments and dislike.

My number one priority in my life was my family. I knew that my strength was a drag for all of you. That I talked too much. That I opened up with everything that came through my mind and heart, and that this was too much for you kids. You really didn't want to hear it all. But I wanted to share it all so I did it anyway. Other than the men in my life, I didn't have the time to spend with other people. Friendship was not important to me because I wanted my children to be my friends. That was a pretty big order, I guess. Probably impossible. But the word "friend" meant nothing to me. I wanted to share my feelings, thoughts, pains, and successes with my children, not with outsiders. Was it too much to ask to share my feelings and thoughts with you kids? I was going to do it anyway—if it drove you away, then that was your choice.

Richard, Mike, and I with
"Old Faithful"

1967

Jackie, learning to fly

Midway through summer flight

Posing with President of Jeppeson

Pinning Jackie's corsage

After our wedding

Ready to leave in Suburban

Part of Lincoln City commune group

Commune's last days
(Paul, center with two sons)

Evan and I in front of
A-frame barn, Brush Prairie, WA

Jackie with grandchildren,
Ezra (toddler) and Evan (newborn)

My sons and I in Amsterdam (with YWAM)

Playing music and preaching, Amsterdam's Central Station

PART THREE

Role Reversal

I dreamed a concrete sidewalk stretched before me in a straight line to the horizon. Next to the sidewalk, an army of charcoal gray, wood-shingled houses, all with steps and wide porches stood shoulder to shoulder. They reminded me of Oakland homes built in the early 20th century. The sky was the color of white ash, nondescript. There were no cars on the street, no movement from the houses, only an eerie absence of sound. It was neither cold nor warm.

As I approached an intersection, I saw an old woman bending over a metal trash bin, her upper body rooting around in its maw. I thought she must be homeless. She stood abruptly and turned towards me, arms held aloft with treasure, her thin, white hair, floating static-wild around her face. She was dressed in a tattered, flowered shift, or maybe a night-gown. Over that she wore a bright pink sweater, wrongly buttoned, so that one side hung down further than the other. Greasy looking stains dribbled down the fronts of both sweater and dress, beneath which her bare legs ended in filthy, baby blue slippers.

When she saw me, her eyes widened with delight, and she reached out to show me what she'd pulled out of the trash. "Look what a great deal I got!" she said, laughing.

With a start, I realized she was my mother.

I sat straight up in bed, gasping for air. All day, all week, I couldn't shake the dream. I had a terrible, terrible feeling I'd seen the future.

❖

It began in early 1997 when my mother joined the Peace Corps and went to Sri Lanka to teach English. At seventy-four, she was one of the oldest volunteers ever allowed into the Corps. Initially, though she'd jumped through every flaming bureaucratic hoop—multiple physical exams, tests, psychological evaluations, letters of recommendation, and counseling sessions—they had declined her application. When I visited, all she talked about was the Peace Corps.

"These people are stupid! They just keep asking for more: dentists and doctors, tests and more tests. They think that just because I'm older I can't keep up." She gripped a thick stack of letters and shook it in my direction as evidence.

"Most women your age wouldn't keep up. The Corps just wants to be sure you'll be safe," I said. "And cover their asses," I added. She didn't smile.

"The whole thing makes me so angry! All this red tape and no common sense."

The Peace Corps had no idea whom they were dealing with, but I did, and I never doubted they would eventually let her in. Six months later, she won her appeal.

Over the years, after she brought us back from Amsterdam and through my divorce from Eric and second marriage, my mother and I had mellowed toward one another: she criticized me less and, in return, I argued with her less. Somewhere along the way, I had made the decision that if I couldn't have the kind of mother I wanted, I would do my best to accept the kind of mother I had. I suspect she'd decided the same, in reverse. And when she asked me to handle her business while she was away, I accepted. Little did I know that this temporary arrangement would become a more extensive, permanent reversal of roles—that who my mother was and who we were to each other would be forever changed.

As her departure date approached, she gave me—repeatedly—lists of instructions. She introduced me to bankers, attorneys, and the managers at her apartment building. She made duplicates of everything and put them in clearly labeled folders, one for her file cabinet and one for mine. Lists haunted my days and floated through my dreams at night. What if something happened to her in Sri Lanka? Except for an emergency number for one of the Corps' administrative offices, the only way to contact her would be by letter: fragile, tissue-thin pieces of paper traveling up to six weeks to reach her.

But, in my heart, I believed nothing bad would happen. My mother was fearless and impervious to normal frailties. We, her children, were of that same stock: fifth-generation Californians, descendants of pioneers who had, for the promise of gold, braved the dangerous cross-country, wagon-wheeled journey; we had traversed the Oregon trail, then moved down to California, settling in San Francisco and the surrounding hills. Our family legend portrayed us as a fiercely independent, spontaneous, strong-willed people with a propensity for alcoholism and violent tempers. We also boasted an equal share of teetotalers and teachers. My mother represented, perhaps, the best of both flanks, having lived her entire life in defiance of limits and on her own terms. She declared she would outlive her children, had, in fact, repeated these words often enough that they'd become a mantra, a myth of invincibility.

I threw a bon voyage party for her, renting the community clubhouse for a potluck celebration. Over forty people came, including nearly all our living relatives, many I hadn't seen in ten or fifteen years. Mom wore a soft, white shirt tucked into her favorite plaid capris—comfortable and practical. As a concession to the event, she'd put on makeup, and coral earrings dangled from her earlobes. Her hair, curled around her ears and newly dyed a light strawberry blonde (who knew when she'd be able to dye it again?), shone slightly pink under the florescent lights of the clubhouse, the effect only adding to her girlish glow.

My mother bustled about chatting with her sister and brother, aunts and uncles. Mom's favorite, Aunt Inez, who'd been a missionary in India for thirty years, was there, though she could no longer walk unsupported.

Mom had always spoken with nostalgic longing about the large family gatherings of her youth, and I was thrilled that I could give this to her before she left, could be a part of making her feel loved and special. I gathered everyone together for a toast, filling their glasses with champagne or soda. The adults stood in a semi-circle facing my mother and me, while the children sat at their feet, water from the swimming pool running in tiny rivulets from their bodies onto the checked linoleum floor.

"I'm so proud of my wild, courageous, adventurous mother," I said. "How many of us can even hope to do a fraction of the things in our lifetimes that she has? Here's to Jackie, Teacher Extraordinaire, and a safe, successful journey." We raised our glasses. Mom laughed and cried, overwhelmed by conflicting emotions: joy at seeing so many relatives, yet sadness to realize, given their ages, that she would probably never see some of them again; excitement for the adventure on which she was about to embark, tinged with apprehension. I put my arm around her shoulders, feeling large next to her small frame. Cameras flashed.

Later, she said, "That was one of the best moments of my life."

After her departure, she wrote every day. She wrote about the friendly people, bad roads, and her constant fear of falling and breaking a hip. She wrote about political upheaval. From the training school she was attending prior to her teaching assignment, she could hear the nearby thunder of explosives and rattle of gunfire.

A postcard written soon after her arrival said:

Cows, sheep, and hogs walk the same roads I walk to go to my school, which lasts for many hours. No desks, no closets—living out of suitcases. It's hard. Primitive villages. No phones, no bank, no transportation. We're in boot camp ... 55 hours to get here, foreign food, eat with hands, 15 shots (10 more to go). No way to use my computer. Terrible roads. Packed highways. Dangerous.

She was frightened all the time, shaken by cultural differences and the burgeoning war. But she braved it out, writing affirmations to herself on scraps of paper.

You are not a victim! You have choices. ... The Peace Corps in Sri Lanka wasn't set up for you! You can take back your power and control your own life. ... This is a beautiful country with wonderful, friendly, caring people. They just need to know what your goals are and if that isn't enough, go get it for yourself!

I first found myself in the position of "being" Mom a few weeks after she left, when Richard was arrested on a DUI repeat offender charge and put in jail. For years I had criticized my mother for always rescuing—in my opinion, enabling—my brothers, so they rarely experienced the consequences of their actions. She had also rescued me financially several times, but I excluded myself from criticism because I had used her help constructively. If I felt pangs of hypocrisy, I pushed them aside; I was a responsible adult who took care of my family and never got in trouble with the law. But now I needed to act in her stead, regardless of my feelings about it. So I hired our family attorney (his minimum retainer was ten thousand dollars) to get my brother out of jail. The attorney had good relationships with the local judges, and Richard was released on his own recognizance.

That was only the beginning.

The tenant to whom my mother had lease-optioned a duplex refused to make payments. She claimed my brother David, who lived in the other half of the duplex, was terrorizing her, that he called her names and repeatedly cut off her electricity. He denied the charges. But I knew David had a dark side to him and wasn't sure whom to believe. I met with the tenant but, soon after, in a confrontation with my brother, she called the police. David, who had a police record in Santa Clara, ran— jumping over a fence to evade them—and hid out at our family's property in La Honda, where Mike lived. The tenant filed suit in Federal Civil Rights Court naming David, my mother, and me as defendants, claiming we conspired to deprive her of her civil rights because she was a Chinese woman.

Michael's ex-wife was also headed to prison, leaving their four daughters behind. I offered to let one of the girls live with me for a while; she and my daughter were only a few months apart and they could share a room. That was the best I could do.

Then, because both my mother's name and my name were on the title to my townhouse, the County placed a lien on it in a mix-up regarding taxes owed on another property my mother had sold.

Each of these problems required phone calls, letters, appointments, and money to resolve. Lots of time. Lots of effort. How did my mother live like this! I didn't want to be like her, let alone *be* her, even temporarily. Every day I asked how I'd allowed myself to get in this position. But I knew: I wanted to be a good daughter, I wanted my mother's approval and trust, and frankly there was no one else in the family who could and would do it.

It wasn't as if that was all I had to do. I was forty-two and in the midst of my second divorce, a single mother (again) with a toddler, a learning-challenged eleven-year-old, and two grown but not yet adult boys: Ezra and Evan, now twenty-one and nineteen. I felt so burdened with family and work responsibilities, so absorbed with my own healing and personal growth, that if I had not agreed to take care of her finances and property while she was away, I would barely have registered my mother's absence. I felt I was doing a piss-poor job of everything.

Six weeks after she reached Sri Lanka, my mother's letters stopped. It was unusual, but I wrote it off to Sri Lanka's unreliable mail service. The letter I finally received, two weeks later, alarmed me.

> *July 22nd. I took a train to Kandy, found my way to Perideniya English Teachers' Training College, and arranged my housing for my two-year commitment to the Peace Corps. That night I fell: six stitches in my head, cracked ribs, black and blue all over, and a whiplash. I spent nine days in the hospital under 24-hour supervision. I've fallen twice since then. My balance is shot.*

For the first time in my life, I worried about my mother's well being. I worried about the care she'd received in a Sri Lankan hospital. I worried about her being so far away. But she wrote that she wanted to stay.

Two months after arriving in Sri Lanka, she completed "boot camp," was sworn into the Corps, and began teaching at the English Teachers' Training College in Perideniya. But in her letters—scrawled handwriting, shaky and tremulous, over the parchment-thin airmail stationery— she questioned whether she could continue in the face of the growing violence, and whether it had been a good idea to come, at all. She loved the people—so warm and generous—but she was afraid all the time. I wrote that maybe she should come home.

Eight months into her two-year commitment, my mother told the Corps she was done. The bus she rode on her way to the administration office for her exit interview was just entering Colombo when the separatist Tamil Tigers detonated a bomb in Colombo's business district, shattering windows, killing eighteen people and wounding 100 more. The military stopped the bus and forced everyone to disembark. Not knowing their language, my mother understood only that there had been a terrorist attack. She didn't know what to do. A man who had also been on the bus noticed her distress and arranged for her transportation back to the college. Without the exit interview, the Peace Corps granted my mother a "Medical Separation" and sent her home.

When she came home, Mom seemed shrunken, as if inches had been cut from her stature, as though something was broken. She began to isolate herself in her apartment. She could still be outgoing, talkative, and feisty, but there was less a tone of "I can do anything" in her speech and manner. Her sense of defeat upset her self-image, as well as my sense of who she was as my mother and I as her daughter.

They say that when people have Alzheimer's, they return to a child-like state. Not true. A child, though she may not be able to talk or feed herself or understand how the world works, is always in a state of expansion. She focuses outward, reaches out with her senses, and grasps the world in her hands. Always learning and growing, a child enchants us with her bright eyes and limitless energy. An Alzheimer's victim, though reverting to childish behaviors, is nothing like a child. She focuses deeply inward, grows backwards instead of forwards. Her soul retreats into the womb of oblivion, leaving nothing but an empty husk behind.

A person with Alzheimer's disease is more like a three-year-old child who no longer plays imaginatively, one who has lost interest in books and dolls and exploring the world. Oh, she still needs to be dressed and fed, still has tantrums, hits and cries and grunts out her rage. But soon she forgets how to be three. She forgets how to speak, how to make meaning of words. She forgets she once thought the world an interesting place and sags listlessly in a chair, staring at the wall or the floor, barely bothering to lift her head when someone enters the room. Her body shrinks. She forgets how to run, then walk. Soon she forgets how to feed herself and how to use the toilet. Eventually, she forgets how to swallow and finally, how to breathe.

My mother began referring to things descriptively. Television became The Box With People In It. A bicycle became The Thing With Wheels That You Pump. My brothers became one another, and I usually became Heather, my niece. She knew what these things were, who we were; she just couldn't pair correct nouns with the things or people to which they belonged.

She had always had difficulty remembering names and coming up with the right words for things, so at first none of us paid attention when Mom complained about her memory. The doctor told her, "Don't worry. You're just experiencing the normal memory loss of old age." Unconvinced, she went to a second doctor. He said the same thing.

"I know something's wrong," she argued.

Finally she demanded a brain scan. The results were normal, except for small infarcts (areas of dead tissue due to tiny, imperceptible strokes)—nothing out of the ordinary for a woman her age. But Mom waved the report in my face. "See, I knew it. I have brain damage."

She didn't tell me she'd also gone to Stanford in April of 2000, taken a series of tests, and been diagnosed with Alzheimer's. Not until after I moved her to an assisted living facility and cleaned out her apartment did I discover the truth, finding the papers she'd signed acknowledging the diagnosis and promising to discuss it with her family. A promise she didn't keep. Instead, my mother clung to the notion that her memory loss wouldn't get worse.

I visited her once a week, after work on Fridays. The rest of the week, I telecommuted to my San Jose office from my home in the Sierra Foothills, where I'd moved with my two youngest children after she returned from Sri Lanka. It seemed to me that, more and more, our conversations turned to what would happen with her estate after she died. Most people I knew with aging parents had to approach the topic of estate planning with delicacy and tact. But my mother, never particularly polite, had lost all patience for social niceties, such as "Hello," "Goodbye," and "How are you doing?"

"I want you to see where I keep everything," she insisted.

"Mom," I said, exasperated, "do we have to talk about death every time I visit? Can't we just chat like normal people?"

Ignoring me, she got up from her armchair—a yard-sale find with a hideous orange upholstered seat that she loved—and headed for the four-drawer file cabinet in her office. I trailed after her, sighing. She slid open the top drawer and retrieved the first folder, what I called her "death folder," containing step-by-step instructions for what to do when she died, pertinent addresses, phone, and account numbers:

1. Call the UC Berkeley number to have them pick up my body (donated for scientific research).

2. Call my sister and other relatives.

3. Go to the bank and clean out my safe deposit box. Put any money not in the trust into the trust account.

4. Order 50 death certificates.

5. Call life insurance companies.

She'd even written her own obituary and listed the phone numbers for the advertising departments of the San Francisco Chronicle and the San Jose Mercury News.

She put everything in a trust, named me Alternate Trustee, gave me full power of attorney, and added me as co-signer on all her bank accounts. In spite of the growing evidence to the contrary, I still wanted to believe my mother invincible.

Sure, she's not as strong as she once was, I reasoned, and she needs more help than she did before. But that's normal, right? She's just obsessing. She'll be fine.

I didn't pay attention to what I viewed as ranting. I had a copy of the folder; I didn't need to memorize its contents. I knew where everything was. Besides, she was too young for all of this.

One afternoon, I left work early and accompanied her to an ophthalmologist appointment. She drove. She'd always been an aggressive driver, but now she sped through intersections muttering, "Quick, before the light turns," as the lights shifted from yellow to red. She misjudged distances, cutting off other drivers who honked angrily.

"Mom, slow down." I gripped the door handle and held my breath as she rolled through a stop sign and turned left in front of an oncoming car.

When we made it back to her apartment, I took her keys. "You scared me half to death today. It's not safe for you to drive anymore. Mike, David, and I can take you anywhere you want to go."

"You can't take my car away!"

She yelled and cried and swore, "Goddamn you!" and tried to grab the keys out of my hand. But I refused to give in. When she went to the bathroom, I hid the keys in the bottom of her linen closet between layers of sheets. My heart thumped so hard I thought she might hear it from behind the closed bathroom door. Later, I called Mike, told him what I'd done and where the keys were. "You have to help," I said.

David went to her apartment and returned her keys. A week later, she collided her Taurus with another car in the apartment parking lot. The police confiscated her keys and her license, but she remembered I had taken them first and, as long as she had the power of speech, claimed I had robbed her of her independence.

I began to notice other things. A rent check had been written incorrectly: the hand-written dollar amount didn't match the number. And it wasn't the only check like that. I couldn't understand how the bank had been processing them.

"Mom, would you like me to take over paying your bills?"

"Oh, yes," she said with obvious relief, which surprised me. I'd expected resistance.

Next, she had trouble opening cans and couldn't operate the microwave. She seemed thinner. I arranged for additional childcare and began driving down twice a week to do her grocery shopping and check in on her. I bought nutritious, easy open, easy eat foods: yogurt, cottage cheese, fruit, Ensure, her favorite ice creams, and salad dressings. I opened cans and put the contents in plastic containers, filled Ziploc bags with individual servings of salad, and dispensed her medications into a divided container labeled with days of the week. I programmed her phone with her children's and emergency phone numbers so she could phone anyone with a push of one button. She called me almost every day.

"Mom's going downhill," I told my brothers. "You need to visit her more often, keep an eye on her. It's too hard on me from so far away, and I have my own children to take care of."

"She's fine," they said, brushing off my concerns. And when they visited her, she *was* fine. Later, I would learn that in the early to mid stages of the disease, people with Alzheimer's are masters at hiding their confusion and memory loss. Mom had become wily.

The next time I took my mother to the doctor's office for a routine checkup, I told him I had concerns about her ability to care for herself.

"Can you tell me what day it is?" he asked her.

"Yes," she said, and looked at the ceiling.

"What day is it?"

She paused. "Monday. No, Tuesday." It was Wednesday.

"Can you tell me the name of the President?"

"Yes, George Bush," she said proudly. "I like that Rice woman."

"Would you look at the clock and tell me what time it is?"

"Clock?" She stared at the doctor, her brows pulled together in a puzzled expression.

"Yes, it's on the wall." He pointed.

She looked at the large analog clock on the wall and fidgeted. "I want to go now."

"Wait a minute, Mom," I said. "Let the doctor finish."

He gave her a piece of paper and asked her to draw a picture of the clock. She put the pen to paper and drew a squiggly line. She stood up. "I want to go. Now."

The doctor nodded, wrote something on his pad, and handed it to me. It said, "She shouldn't be living alone."

On the way back to her apartment, I broached the subject. "Mom, the doctor told me it's not safe for you to live alone. You need to be where someone can look after you all the time."

"I can move into the Tall Building," she said, referring to the tower, the tallest building in Valley Village, the senior complex in which she lived. Because the rooms didn't have kitchens, she believed they offered assisted living.

"No, Mom. I checked. Valley Village has a nurses' station where they can take your blood pressure and give you your medications, but you have to go get them. And in the tower, the residents eat in the cafeteria, but they have to get there on their own. They don't offer assistance."

"Yes they do," she said, refusing to discuss it further.

I called my brother Terry, in Los Angeles. "The day you move Mom to a rest home is the day she dies," he said. "Don't do it."

I didn't call John or Richard. John, because he hadn't talked to Mom in years and would have nothing to do with her. Richard, because, though he was back in California, he was drinking heavily again and became belligerent and mean when drunk. I called Mike. "You'll never get Mom to move," he said. David said, "No way."

So, I procrastinated. I hired a woman to check in on her daily, paid Meals on Wheels to deliver dinners, and if she didn't call me I called her. When I saw she'd forgotten to take her medicine, I brought it to the nurse's station for them to dispense. If she didn't arrive by 11:00 a.m. each day, they called to remind her.

In October 2003, I was working in my home office and absently answered the phone after two rings, my mind on a FileMaker Pro script coding problem.

"I'm calling from the Santa Clara Hospital Emergency Room. Is this Linda Peterson, Jacquelyn Carr's daughter?"

"Yes," I said, instantly alert. "What happened? Is my mom okay?"

"Your mother fell and cut open her scalp. We had to staple the wound shut. She'll be fine, but she's disoriented. We'd like to keep her 24 hours for observation. "

"Of course."

"We'll need your signature."

"It'll take me a few hours. I'll be there as soon as I can," I said.

I learned more after I arrived at the hospital. Someone had seen her walking through her apartment complex with blood seeping onto her collar at the back of her neck, her hair all matted with dried blood, unaware of her injury.

When I stood at her bedside, she smiled and said, "I don't need anyone. I took care of myself."

Later, I pieced together what had happened. She had passed out while at her bathroom sink. When she came to, she lay on the floor in a pool of blood. Her head hurt. She had dabbed the back of her head with a damp washcloth and then lain down on her bed to take a nap. The next morning, she'd gotten up, dressed, and was on her way to the community room for her ritual mid-morning cookies, when she was stopped by "that nice lady" who called an ambulance.

I stayed with her for several days while I tried to figure out the best option for her care. She had enough money, I reasoned, so I made arrangements for a live-in caretaker. Her apartment was tiny: 500 square feet, with a bedroom, small bathroom, living room, and a miniature half-kitchen. She had used the bedroom as an office and slept on the daybed in the living room, so I set up a folding bed in the office for the caretaker and hoped for the best.

My mother threw the first caretaker's bags into the hallway and locked the door when the poor woman went out to retrieve them. The second caretaker lasted two days. "She won't let me give her a bath, and she hit and scratched me this morning when I refused to let her leave the apartment," she said over the phone.

I sighed. "I'll be down in the afternoon."

I tried to explain it again. "Mom, if you don't let someone take care of you here, I'm going to have to move you to an assisted living facility."

"I won't leave here. You can't make me!" She stomped her foot, which in spite of the situation made me smile.

"Yes, Mom, I can. And I will, if you don't let someone live here and take care of you."

"No! Why can't *you* do it? Or Cat. Cat can stay," Mom said. She had taken a liking to Richard's wife, and since Cat had expressed willingness to help, I asked her if she'd stay with Mom four days each week. I'd stay the other three.

After a week or two of this arrangement, Cat called. "I found Mom walking outside the apartment in her underwear at three o'clock this morning. I'm not going to be able to do this."

So, that is that, I thought, and made arrangements for my mother to move to Ralston Village in Belmont. It was among the few facilities I visited that didn't smell of urine, which seemed to me to indicate a higher level of care. And I thought she might be more accepting of the place because its name was similar to Valley Village, where she had lived for the past three years.

It had drawbacks. It was expensive, and they required all dementia residents to share rooms. The Administrator told me that people with dementia remain more functional with increased social contact. While I believed her, I had doubts about my mother. But they did have an empty room at present, and she'd have it to herself for a while, giving her time to adjust.

On the day of her move, I conspired with Mike to take her to the park and then for ice cream while I transferred essential clothing, some of her photo albums, and a few pictures from her walls to her new room. When all was ready, under the pretense of visiting a friend, he took her to Ralston Village. Once inside, he left her with the staff. He walked out, crying.

Although Mike had become convinced that Mom needed full-time care, Terry told me I'd made a mistake. Richard told me I was overreacting. David said, "Mom can take care of herself. She does just fine." Alone in bed at night, I wept, second-guessing myself.

The door clanged shut as I entered the dementia ward two days later. I flinched at the sound. It was almost lunchtime, and I found my mother in the cafeteria, which doubled as the "Great Room" between meals. The Administrator had counseled me to give my mother a couple of days to settle in before visiting, and I approached her with a great deal of trepidation. How would she respond? Would she be angry? Did she like her room? What would she say?

"Hi Mom," I said, settling into the chair next to her. "How're you doing?" She turned, face tightening and eyes narrowing to match her compressed lips. She wore her favorite sweater. The staff had combed her hair, secured her bangs to the side with a childish hair clip that matched her scarlet sweater, and applied blue eye shadow and mascara—making her look, I thought, like an old doll. She gazed at me only a moment before turning away, shifting in her chair so her back was to me. "C'mon, Mom. This is a nice place. You and I can go for walks in the garden. It's beautiful out there, and once you get to know the other residents, you'll like it."

She kept her back to me and said nothing. At a table across the room, four women were pasting cutout shapes onto colored construction paper. An attractive older black woman sang to herself. Drool ran unchecked from the slack lips of a white-haired man slouching in a wheelchair at the end of the table where we sat. I put my hand on my mother's shoulder. "I love you, Mom. I didn't have a choice."

"I want to go home," she told the opposite wall.

"This is your home, now. You can't stay in your apartment. You need twenty-four-hour care. I know you don't agree, but I wish you could understand that we have to keep you safe."

"I want to go home! Nothing but dead people here!" She indicated the man at the end of the table.

I didn't reply. My stomach tightened into an ache. I tried changing the subject, making small talk about my job, the kids, the weather—anything I could think of to bridge the awkwardness between us. She refused to speak to me.

When lunch arrived, I said goodbye and walked down the linoleum-floored hall to her room. The lights were off, the blinds shut tight, just as they had been in her apartment. I snapped on the overhead light. Her clothing, which I'd organized in her drawers and hung in her closet, had been pulled out of their places and draped over the backs of chairs or stacked on the unoccupied bed across from hers. The pictures I'd placed on the dresser, hoping they would help her feel more at home, had been stuffed into the drawer of her nightstand. Sighing, I put her clothing away. I left the pictures in the drawer. Next time, I'd bring a familiar afghan and a couple of photo albums.

Before I left, I stopped by to see the Administrator. "How do you think she's doing?" I asked.

"Well, she's sure fast," she said.

"What do you mean?"

"When anyone goes through the outer doors, she sneaks up and tries to slip out behind them. She's made it out a couple of times. And let me tell you, your mom can run." She chuckled. "That woman has wheels instead of feet! She almost made it out to the street last time."

"The street?" I said, picturing her running in front of a car.

"Oh, don't worry," the woman said. "We'd never let her get that far." She patted my arm. "This is normal. She'll adjust, trust me." There was something about this woman I disliked: she smiled too broadly, her red lips forced into a wide grin, like an insurance salesman, assuring and patronizing at the same time.

On my way out I met a slim woman, about my mother's age, with stylish gray hair. She wore a beige trench coat and carried a black leather purse on her arm. "My daughter's coming to take me home today," she said.

"That's nice," I said. "Where do you live?"

"Oh!" she said, her eyes brightening as she unclasped her purse. "It's in here somewhere." She riffled through the purse, which was stuffed with small scraps of paper, plastic bangles, and several wrinkled 4x6 photographs.

"Well, give your daughter a big hug when she comes, okay?" I said.

"Oh, I will," she said happily.

We would have many variations of that conversation over the next few months. Martha, as I learned was her name, haunted the daytime corridors of Ralston Village—always wearing the same beige coat and carrying the same black purse, waiting for the daughter who would never arrive.

Time passed. Mom continued to be angry, refusing to accept her situation. And how could I blame her? When she first moved in, the Village's residency numbers were down and though she had the room to herself, I always knew that she'd have to share it. But when they tried to bring in a roommate, my mother attacked the bewildered woman, scratching and kicking. They moved the woman and warned me that my mother couldn't stay if she wouldn't consent to a roommate.

During this time, Mike and David visited only once, Richard not at all. Mike told me he cried when he saw her, and I figured that David and Richard couldn't bear to see her like that either. So, it's hard, I thought. I cry every time, too. I hate it, too. But I go. I go because I don't want to abandon her. Cowards!

Five months into Mom's stay, I got a call from the Administrator. "Your mother's had an accident. We had her transported to the Redwood City Kaiser Hospital."

"What do you mean, 'had an accident'? What happened?" I began shaking as adrenaline surged through my body.

"She was trying to carry a bundle of clothing out of her room when she apparently tripped and fell. She may have broken her wrist or arm."

"I'll be there as soon as I can." I hung up, dialed Michael's number, and left a message—he was probably at work—and made the long drive to Redwood City.

At the hospital, my mother was sleeping, knocked out by an intravenous cocktail of morphine and other painkillers. Her arm was immobilized and bound to her chest. While I waited for the doctor to arrive, I studied her. Deep creases etched her forehead, and her eyes were squeezed shut, like a child pretending to sleep. I softly called her name, but she didn't respond. Every now and then she gave a stuttering breath and moaned. I stroked her brow, trying vainly to smooth out the creases, and murmured to her that things would be okay, the doctor would be in soon. She couldn't hear me; I was only comforting myself.

When the doctor arrived, he showed me her X-rays. As she fell, she'd reached out her hand, palm extended, to catch herself, the full weight of her body colliding with the floor on the fragile point of her wrist. The bones, weakened by osteoporosis, had shattered like glass. She needed immediate surgery.

Though they were able to reconstruct her wrist, she was no longer able to follow rehabilitation instructions. Her hand, held protectively close to her chest, curled into a useless claw as though clutching her heart.

To be closer to her, I found a job in Martinez, moved to my boyfriend's house in Napa (six months sooner than we'd planned), and transferred my mother to the Berkshire, an assisted living facility ten minutes from where we lived.

The Berkshire was ideal. It was more affordable than Ralston Village, Mom had a room of her own, and the halls were carpeted and wallpapered in soothing colors. Although the place sometimes smelled of urine, the staff did their best to keep the residents clean and engaged in activities.

I tied her closet shut so she couldn't remove her clothes, and did all her laundry myself. She calmed down and even let me hang a poster with pictures from Sri Lanka and bring photo albums for her to look at. I spent time with her nearly every day, taking her for walks around and around the halls of the Berkshire, like an indoor track. She would stop at every light switch, flicking it obsessively up and down, up and down, until I could distract her and get her moving again. After a while, except for brief moments of lucidity, she no longer spoke or knew who I was. I believed she thought I was one of the caretakers at the Berkshire, the one who came to take her on walks. But I couldn't be sure. Having lost the ability to recognize hunger or to remember when she ate, she got fat.

The mother I loved and hated was gone. In her place was a stranger. Yet because she was in my mother's form, I cared for her as though she were a disabled daughter. I'd sob in the car on my way home, exhausted from grieving the death of my mother, who was not dead yet, and tired of putting my own life on hold. I wished she would just go ahead and get it over with. She would have hated it, had she known, that this was what she'd become. Still, every time I visited I hoped to see that spark in her eyes, the one that told me my mother was still in there, behind those milky blue irises.

JACKIE

Since 1923, when I was born, I made records of 42 addresses where I lived. I kept records so that I could go back and recreate the many, varied lives I lived. I'd been to more than 90 different countries, done everything I ever wanted to do, including flying '99er Juliet and, because of my records, I could name every place I ever lived, every school I ever attended, every job I ever had, and the people I met.

But aging was not easy. The loss of balance, falling, arthritis, body aches, and hearing loss. Each year, it got worse. But the worst of all was the fear—my brain damage. I didn't want to drive anymore. I got lost easily, couldn't name streets, lost my directions, couldn't remember names, and had lost my ability to count numbers for paying bills.

I made mistakes, like the time I tried to fly to visit Terry and missed my plane. I went into a complete panic. I would wake up in the middle of the night, panicked because I couldn't find legal documents or the records of the properties purchased from Terry. I imagined you trying to settle my estate with the IRS without the records. Eventually, I would find the papers. There were also the lawsuits on the Bismarck property, and our civil case against the San Jose Police, the defense case for David. I couldn't keep it together in my mind.

I felt old, worse than I had ever felt, and only safe at Valley Village. I expected to live there permanently. I was much healthier than most of the seniors I knew, but many of them had better memories. My records took the place of memory. I envied those who had great memories, but I wouldn't trade my experiences for "talking" when I could read about everything I'd done, everywhere I'd traveled, and all the people I'd met. I just wanted it both ways.

It felt like I was getting older by the month. I needed lots of help. I did value the times you helped me. I respected the fact that you had your own life to live and any time you gave to me was frosting on the cake. But I was scared, all the time. I felt like I had no family. My kids were scattered all over—Terry in Los Angeles, Richard in Washington, you up in the mountains, and David in Susanville. Mike was the only one within driving distance. When I didn't hear from him, I phoned, but nobody answered.

I felt strongly that I loved my children more than anything else in my life. More than any man. My life was not about money, although you all saw it that way. I just wanted to be self-sufficient and able to take care of myself. The great Depression and WWII taught some of us to be frugal. It served me well. Did my children benefit from it? I thought so.

I didn't run around wishing I had done it all "better." You have already learned some of these parenting "mistakes" and, if you are like I was, you will do the best you can and let go. Regrets are empty.

I never believed in religion or saying I'm sorry or having regrets. I expressed my feelings in the moment. It seemed more honest to me. Every parent wishes they could be a better parent.

I wished I had focused more on positives. Terry was the most intelligent of my sons. You took responsibility as the executor of my estate. As I approached my eightieth birthday, I felt that things were in control and, except for fears about memory loss, I experienced a great peace of mind. I wished that during your lives I had voiced these kinds of "joys" in my life rather than my anxieties. I knew that part of my life had been anxiety which I often dumped on my children, and I wished I had expressed more positives with you when you were young.

What Would
My Mother Do?

When I realized Mom could no longer process numbers or write checks, I took her financial records home with me. (At the time, she was still in her apartment at Valley Village, and I was living on my two-acre homestead in the Sierra Foothills.) But when I reviewed her bank statements, things didn't add up. Or, more accurately, I didn't want to believe what I was seeing. I stared at the numbers again. Then I called the bank. When our Personal Representative came on the line, the woman's voice was warm and confident and professional; I'd never met her, but I pictured a thirty-something blonde in a power suit sitting at a spotless, cherry wood desk. I sat on my worn, plaid couch, a pile of papers strewn over the outdated oak coffee table in front of me.

"I'm seeing a large transfer every month, ranging from nine thousand to thirteen thousand dollars, from my mother's main checking account to her second account in Los Angeles," I said. "Who's been initiating those transfers?"

"Her son, Terry Carr," came the quick reply.

"He's not a signer on her primary account. I am. Tell me, how has he transferred the money?"

"Well ... let me see ..." Her keyboard clacked in the background. "We have a Power of Attorney for Terry, dated April of 2001, authorizing him access to finalize a real estate loan."

"Did it give him any powers beyond that loan?" I could hear my voice rising with disbelief and outrage.

"Um ... it doesn't appear–"

"Who, on your side, authorized the transfers?

"Well ... uh, I did–"

"I can't believe this! Are you telling me that you've allowed my brother to siphon money from our mother's account for over a *year*?"

"Uh..."

"He has no authorization to access her money. None, whatsoever. You've assisted my brother in the illegal transfer of funds. And it stops. Now!" I pictured myself storming into her office and slapping her unblemished, thirty-something cheeks. It was a good thing she was a three-hour drive away.

"Ms. Peterson–"

"No. This is *your* fault. I've got to sit down and figure out how much he took. You'll be hearing from me."

"Ms. Peterson–"

I hung up, sat back on the couch breathing heavily, and stared out the window at the spreading oaks on the hillside above my home. Shit. I should have known. As Mom's memory started to go, she had warned me, repeatedly: "Don't let Terry take my money." She'd written it in countless emails and letters. She didn't trust him—that's why I would be Trustee, not him. And I'd failed before I'd even begun.

A couple of years before, Terry had gotten in trouble with the IRS and needed to shelter his assets, so he'd convinced my mother to buy his Wilshire Boulevard condominium, which he was supposed to be renting back from her. He promised it would end up costing her nothing: he would make all the mortgage, home owners' association, property tax, and insurance payments—totaling nearly six thousand a month—and purchase the property back from her as soon as he was "back on his feet." Mom passionately hated the IRS. So, of course, she had also given him a loan to pay them off. All this, even though he'd previously borrowed—

and failed to repay—a hundred thousand dollars. I'd reminded her that she didn't trust him, that she'd lost money the last time she'd sheltered his property from the IRS. I told her it wasn't a good idea. But she did it anyway. She didn't trust him *and* couldn't say no to him.

I felt some sympathy for Terry. I knew things hadn't been going well. Not that long ago, he'd been a successful Hollywood director and producer, with movie credits such as *On Golden Pond, Jagged Edge,* the 1976 remake of *Hong Kong, The Boost,* and *Predator 2.* But his career had stalled in '91, after he'd argued with co-producer Michael Douglas and walked off the set of the Van Damme movie, *Double Impact.* Blacklisted, he'd had a hard time finding work. He put everything he owned, and much more, into producing a couple of low-budget movies that went straight to video—the last, *Innocents,* in 2000. Other than that, he'd not worked in ten years, and I was pretty sure he made nothing from the movies he'd produced.

How would my mother handle this situation? That was the only question I had to consider right now. Mom would want, in spite of her warnings to me, to continue helping him out. I knew this. Yet, she'd said, "Don't let him take my money." I would have to confront him. First, though, I had to figure out the extent of his embezzlement.

Two days later, after going through all the files and bank statements, the figure had grown to just under a quarter of a million dollars.

I waited until the kids were at school and I had the house to myself before I phoned. Terry was my big brother, twelve years older than I, and smarter than anyone I'd ever known. He'd gone to Stanford when he was fifteen and earned his Masters degree before he turned twenty-one. He spoke fluent German and had worked in Hollywood since the '60s. When I was twelve, he'd let me be a sidewalk extra in a chase scene filmed in Union Square for a Perry Mason episode, and I still remembered the thrill of it. With everyone—even my mother—he'd always played the role of counselor, doling out convincing, expert advice. Terry had a soft, persuasive voice and was extremely manipulative. I took a deep breath and dialed his number.

After the obligatory and awkward hellos—our family doesn't do chit-chat—I said, "Terry, I don't know any way to say this other than to just say it ... I've been going over Mom's accounts ... you've been stealing from her." He didn't answer right away, pausing just long enough that I wondered if he planned to deny it.

"Borrowed, not stolen. I'm going to pay it back."

Admitting, without admitting, I thought. "Like the hundred grand you already borrowed and never paid back?"

"I still plan on paying it back."

"I'm sure you do. Still, the 'borrowing,' as you call it, is over. I've called the bank."

"Linda, you don't understand. Things have been really hard. There's all the bills. Chika's health insurance alone is eleven-hundred a month ..."

The figure shocked me, though it also made sense. Chika had been a financial and emotional burden to Terry since he'd married her more than twenty years earlier. They'd wanted children, but every time she got pregnant, she miscarried, and she had tried to commit suicide several times. Then she got pregnant with Arieka. The gynecologist had taken the extreme measure of sewing Chika's cervix shut and putting her on bedrest. Finally a father in his fifties, Terry adored Arieka and had centered his life around her. But Chika still battled depression as well as physical illnesses. That's why her insurance was so high. Still, that wasn't Mom's problem. I reminded myself to stay firm.

Terry went on, detailing his litany of ills and difficulties. "Arieka's school is expensive ... she can't go to the public schools around here ... and I have appearances to keep up. When you work in this in-dustry, it's critical to maintain an image of success. If I don't, I'm dead. You don't know what it's like."

"Look, Terry, I know its been hard, but thirteen thousand dollars a month? Really? I know Mom would want you to be able to stay in your home, but she can't afford to support you indefinitely. I'll keep making the house payments for a while—a short while. But you're going to have to start paying rent like you promised."

In some ways, the conversation was going better than expected—at least he hadn't tried to deny or lie about taking the money—but I felt angry at myself for being so soft. I should be yelling at Terry, instead of sitting here speaking politely.

I should sue him, sue the bank, get Mom's money back, I thought, and then almost laughed out loud. Suing Terry would be fruitless, and Mom would never do anything like that anyway. But what would she want *me* to do?

"Just give me some time," he said. "Six months. I've got a new movie deal in the works."

Of course, a new movie deal. "Okay. But I'm serious. Six months."

"Ok. How's Mom?" he said, shifting the subject. I didn't mind; I'd said all I needed to say.

"Not good. I'm worried. Her memory's going really fast."

"She needs vitamins," he said. I've been using this special supplement, a combination of protein and vitamins. It's expensive, but well worth it…." He launched into his well-worn role of big brother, and I listened.

My mother held onto my elbow as we made our way across the spacious office where her attorney sat behind an imposing, dark walnut desk. Behind him, matching floor-to-ceiling bookcases with glass doors reflected our slow progress. He stood and met us halfway, hand extended.

"Jackie, it's good to see you again," he said, his brown eyes warm above his smile. A big man, nearly as substantial as his desk, he towered over my mother, who stared at his hand for a moment before remembering what she was supposed to do. She reached up and grasped his fingers with her left hand. He looked at me over the top of his glasses. I shrugged.

"And you must be Linda. Bryan Lithgow," he said, shaking my hand. He had a firm, warm grip, and I liked him right away. As we settled into the chairs in front of his desk, he asked, "What can I do for you today?"

"We'd like to make a few changes to my mom's trust."

"Oh?" He glanced at my mother, who was toying with an ornate paper clip holder on the edge of the desk.

"First, we want to name me as Trustee," I said. "Right, Mom?" She looked up. "You want me to be Trustee, right?" She looked over at Lithgow, then back at me, and nodded. "And we need to add some of her property. The condominium in L.A. And a couple of bank accounts." I slid a manila folder onto the desk. "Oh, and I'll need a complete power of attorney."

"I want Arieka to be able to stay," my mother said, "until she's twenty-one." Mention of the condominium had caught her attention. Her eyes cleared and her face lit up. "She's such a darling little thing . . . and draws so well. Plays violin, too!" she said to the big man behind the desk.

"Does she?" he said as though interested, but he looked at me with what I took as knowing sympathy. Embarrassed, I looked away, worried he wouldn't consider her competent enough to make the changes. She probably wasn't—I already had two doctors' notes to that effect—but if I couldn't make these changes now, I'd have to prove her incompetence in court. My brothers, particularly Terry, might fight it. Getting the trust changed now would make my life so much easier.

Lithgow watched my mother, who alternated between patting her legs and fiddling with the zipper on her purse. I looked down to see my hands wringing each other. I forced them apart to sit quietly on my lap.

"As long as Terry makes the house payments," I said. "Mom . . . We can write into your trust that Terry and Arieka can stay in the house as long as he pays the rent ... like he said he would." Her brows drew to-gether and her lips pursed. "You can't afford to make his payments for him. Right?"

"Yes, he has to make the payments," she said. I let out my breath. It was an important concession. Terry had convinced her to buy the condo on the grounds that he would cover all the costs. But when I had tried to tell her about his stealing her money, she reacted forcefully—angrily—not at him, but at me for suggesting he would do such a thing. And she continued to insist he was making his payments. I'd given up arguing with her about it.

I understood that she wanted to help him, understood that she want-ed Arieka, her favorite grandchild, to continue living in their home. She had always made sure we had decent places to live, but I had an obliga-tion to protect her from Terry. If she locked the trust into keeping the condo until Arieka was an adult, I feared there wouldn't be enough money for her care.

"Right," Lithgow said. He seemed to have sized things up and made a decision. Offering cookies, coffee, and soda if we wanted to wait, he could have the papers ready for us to sign within an hour. We waited.

When Lithgow returned, I handed the pen to my mother and showed her where to sign. She looked down at the form and paused, seeming confused, until I prompted her a second time to sign her name. "Right here," I said slowly, "Just sign 'Jacquelyn B. Carr.'" She placed the pen on the line where I pointed, and fidgeted in her seat, her eyes flash-ing with agitation.

"Do you need help?" I whispered. She nodded. I placed my hand over hers, feeling the hard knobs of her knuckles and thin flesh of her fingers beneath mine, and began to guide her hand. Then, as though her body memory abruptly awoke, she shook me off, and scratched her name across the page. When she finished signing next to all the *X*s, she looked up happily.

"Can we go now?" she said. I could see Lithgow out of the corner of my eye, watching us.

"Yes, we can go now." We gathered our purses and stood together. The attorney walked us to the door, chatting with my mother and wishing her a good day. Just before we slipped through the doorway, he laid a large hand on my shoulder. I turned to face him. Impatient, my mother continued through to the hall.

"She's lucky to have such a good daughter," he said.

"Thank you," I murmured, and turned to follow my mother before he could see the tears brimming my eyes.

Six months had become ten. Ten months had stretched into twelve, and then eighteen. I would call Terry, and he'd promise to pay something, the HOA fees. He said he'd get the money, but he never did. I offered to help him move and pay his rent if he would find someplace cheaper. But no, he said, I had no idea how dangerous it was in Los Angeles. The gangs and the crime. There was no way they could move. Anything cheaper would put his family in danger. He just needed a little more time. He had a deal brewing. He was in the middle of negotiations. If I would just wait until he turned sixty-two, he'd get social security. Then he could help out.

By this time, Mom was living at Ralston Village. When she broke her wrist, and when she started hitting other residents, she needed special round-the-clock care. That cost extra. Each month, I paid the bills and watched her bank balance plummet. I'd visited some of those places supported by Medicare: they stank of unwashed bodies and urine and depression; they stank of desolation and rotting flesh. Mom had worked hard for her money. She deserved better than that, better than being one of twelve or fifteen helpless old people for every overworked, minimum-wage caretaker. I had no choice.

That's what I told him: "Terry, I have no choice. We have to sell the condo. We need the money to take care of Mom."

"Okay," he said. He sounded resigned, but I didn't trust him.

"I'll give you ten thousand dollars to move," I said, thinking that's what Mom would want me to do. Thinking I was being generous. "That should be enough for first and last and a month or two of rent somewhere." But I worried. How many months would it take for him to find a new place to live? All he had to do was dig in his heels, refuse to show the house. How would I handle everything from so far away? I hired an attorney and sent Terry an official eviction notice.

"We're thinking about moving to Coos Bay, Oregon," he said, the next time I talked to him.

"Oh, it's nice up there. Beautiful area. And the cost of living is a lot lower than L.A."

"I've got a buyer," he said, "for the condo. Professional Iranian guy."

"Really? Have you talked price?"

"Yeah. He agreed to the price you and I talked about. We can do this without a real estate agent." I hesitated. I'd expected him to be cagey, to do everything he could to delay a sale and to stay. Instead, he'd acquiesced. He was actually going to help.

My real estate attorney drew up the paperwork and the whole deal was done by July 1, 2005. There would be enough money to take care of Mom, and it seemed everything was going to work out. I gave Terry the ten grand so they could move and pay rent until he found work up in Oregon. When I talked to him, he sounded upbeat. It was a small community, he said, and the schools had a good reputation. It was quiet. They would be happy there.

When he spent almost the entire amount to purchase a shipping container for their belongings and have it trucked to Oregon, I told him it was unwise not to reserve anything for housing. He said he had everything under control. They were excited. It would be a new chapter in their lives. But when they arrived in the Coos Bay area, they couldn't find a house they liked. They stayed in a motel for a few weeks looking for housing and work, and decided the community was too small. They decided the people were backwards, intolerant of Chika's Japanese almond eyes and skin, intolerant of Arieka's mixed race. No way could Chika and Arieka be comfortable living there.

"Didn't you research the town before moving?" I asked when he phoned.

"We're going down to Ashland," he said. "A university town will be better for us."

"What about your stuff? The shipping container?"

"We'll leave it here until we find something in Ashland. The motel owner is letting us park it."

"Are you going to be okay?"

"We'll be fine."

The call came as I sat in my windowless office, gazing at the dirty wall above my desk and wishing, probably for the millionth time, for something resembling a view to the outside world.

"Line three," the receptionist called through my open door.

"Okay, thanks," I said, punching the blinking button on the phone. "Client Relations. How can I help you?"

"Linda?"

"Yes?"

"It's Vicki."

I hadn't talked to Vicki, my brother John's wife, in a long time. We weren't estranged, but John and my mother were, so our lives just didn't cross paths. For Vicki to call me at work ...

"It's Terry," she said, her voice crisp, controlled. "Linda ... I'm sorry ... I don't know how to say this ... he's dead."

My vision telescoped and narrowed until the room went dark. Black as ink, as though I'd gone suddenly blind. The windowless space pressed against my chest, and it felt as though I was pulling an unbreathable, gel-like liquid into my lungs instead of air, drowning in thick darkness. Gasping. Unable to comprehend. My ears rang. I thought I might faint and pushed my bare feet flat against the floor, cold and hard and real. I pressed the cold, hard phone against my ear until it hurt. Vicki continued. I heard her voice, thin and flat, as through tin can and string.

"That's not all," Vicki continued. "Arieka too ... I'm so sorry ... They were both found dead in their car ... Terry's Jeep ... at the Tower Market gas station, two miles from our house. And Chika ... Chika's missing."

I couldn't speak.

"I'm sorry," Vicki said. "I'm so sorry to have to tell you ... like this."

"What happened?" The words, squeezed from my compressed lungs and into my throat, croaked into the phone.

"We don't know yet. They found them this afternoon. That's all I know."

I was breathing too fast, hyperventilating. I had to slow down, stay present, try not to fall into the black pit that had opened under my desk, beneath my feet. Breathe in. Out. In. Out. Slow, slow, slower. Okay. The desk, the floor felt solid, hard, real again.

"John?" I asked.

"He's devastated. That's why I called instead of him."

"Thanks," I said. "I'll call later. I can't think. I can't breathe." I placed the receiver in the cradle—carefully, gently, slowly, laying the phone to sleep. Then I laid my forehead against the solid hard wood of my desk, threw my arms up and over my head as if to protect myself from the inevitable impact, and sobbed. I sucked in air, but it still felt as though I wasn't getting enough oxygen. My heart was starving.

Terry ... Arieka ... the loss knifed through me, and with it a searing, burning guilt. It was because of me that he—they—were dead.

Terry, Chika, and Arieka had arrived in Ashland and rented an apartment on July 29th. Shortly after, someone saw Terry's Jeep parked by the side of the road and Terry throwing boxes of clothing, family photos, and files over a barbed-wire fence into the pasture on the other side.

Two days later, the three of them were eating lunch in the deli section of Ashland's Market of Choice grocery store when Chika went to the restroom. In the footage from the store's security cameras, Terry is seen nonchalantly walking out of the store with his daughter, getting into the Jeep, and driving away. Chika, not knowing what had happened, went home to their new apartment and waited, finally reporting them missing the following morning.

Terry drove south 275 miles and arrived at the Tower Station in Clearlake Oaks, less than two miles from John and Vicki's house, in the pre-dawn hours of August 1st. He parked in the lot by the side of the store.

It was stifling hot—102 degrees that afternoon—when the store clerk, who had sold Terry snacks and beverages in the morning, noticed the car still parked in the lot and decided to investigate. A shopping cart filled with clothing and personal effects sat beside the Jeep. When he looked inside, he saw car keys dangling from the ignition. In the back, a man and girl seemed to be sleeping. When he couldn't wake them, he called the police.

It took two days to connect the case of the missing man and child in Oregon with the dead man and child in California. It took twenty days for the toxicology report to be completed. In the space between the discovery of their bodies and the coroner's report, we questioned and speculated; police questioned and speculated; newspaper reporters questioned and speculated.

Why had Terry thrown away all their things? Why had he abandoned Chika in Ashland? Why had he driven all the way to Clearlake and then stopped at the Tower Mart? Had he planned to visit John? If so, why hadn't he called? Maybe he'd planned to commit suicide, leaving Arieka for John. Maybe he'd killed them both. What caused their deaths?

According to Dr. Kelly Arthur, Lake County pathologist, Terry died of cardiac dysrhythmia—a heart attack. He conjectured that when Terry suffered the attack, his 212-pound body fell across the sleeping body of his small daughter, who then died from lack of oxygen. One death from natural causes, the other an accident caused by the first.

We, those who were closest to Terry, remained skeptical. Terry was brilliant; he, of all people, would know a way to kill himself without leaving a chemical trace. But he loved Arieka—adored her—too much, some might say. Maybe he couldn't face leaving this world without her. She had clearly died of asphyxiation. Could he have done that to her? Could he have killed her and then himself?

On a Thursday evening, about two weeks before his death, Terry phoned. I was at home. I remember, because I was cooking dinner and felt irritated at the interruption, defensive because I assumed he was calling for money.

"What do you need?" I asked.

"I don't need anything. Just calling to talk." I relaxed, and we chatted for about thirty minutes. He asked about Mom and my kids, asked how I liked my new job. He seemed positive that things would get better. When we hung up, I felt relieved.

Later—after everything—I found out that he'd also called John and Richard and Mike and David that same night. We all remembered it was a Thursday, because he'd called "just to talk," which was out of character; we'd never known him to call without an agenda.

Now, Terry and Arieka were dead. And eight months after their death, on what would have been Arieka's tenth birthday, Chika, alone in Ashland, took her own life.

Some people go through life asking, "What would Jesus—or Buddha—or Gandhi—do?" For me, it is always, "What would my mother have done?" Would she have been willing to pay indefinitely for Terry's housing, bankrupting herself in the process? Would she have given him more than ten thousand dollars? Would she have bought a cheaper house and given it to him? I wrack my heart with these questions.

JACKIE

My most intelligent son, the oldest, was in the wrong business—making movies—a political game of brilliant people. Terry was smart enough, but I felt he was too honest to win that game.

Over the years, when Terry had financial difficulties, he'd ask for my help. In his business, anything less than a hundred thousand was nothing. So, in 2001, I had him sign off his share of my estate, knowing he'd already gotten more than the rest of the family, and I gave him another loan.

I hadn't planned to buy any more property. A few years earlier, I'd ended up with Terry's Hawaii condominium, which had to be sold. But I bought his Los Angeles condominium thinking it would be the last gift I would give in this world.

I felt sad that I gave so much to my sons, and they didn't seem to benefit from it. I gave away as much as I could and still support myself. Most adults—including you—told me I made poor decisions by helping my children so much. But I couldn't bear to let them lose their homes, go to prison, or end up suicides like my mother. They were all alive! To have six children, all able to stay alive without tragedy, has to be some measure of success.

When Terry and Chika, a fifty-nine-year-old father and forty-six-year-old mother, couldn't support themselves, I couldn't let them lose their home; I didn't have what it would take to put them out on the streets. Terry had no credit, the IRS was against him, and his wife was not well. Should I have let her commit suicide? She'd already tried three times. They had the gift of that five-year-old, darling little girl, but Terry couldn't work. He tried, but hadn't had a job in years, and I didn't expect Terry would ever pay his debts to me.

Still, I thought he'd be able to pay rent to cover the costs and was glad I didn't have to sign or deal with anything connected to it except to receive a statement each month. I made it clear that if he didn't make the payments, I would sell the house and let them live with whatever they could.

I didn't have the heart to let Terry sink, with his Miracle Baby and his wife who spent lots of money. Even the car Terry drove was in my name. But I had nightmares—long, horror sweats at night—in which Terry couldn't pay for his house. I didn't know what he would do. Chika never worked more than a few days in her life. I felt that she was a good mother, and I wished she could get her brother, who was rich, to help—but the two had been enemies ever since she left her family and came to the States.

When the neurologist confirmed my memory loss, all I could think was, "Now, I must pay attention. I have to stop taking care of all my children." And I told everyone that when the time came, and I couldn't manage financial problems, that you would be my executor, that you would be trustworthy and fair. You had learned to support yourself, had your own home and security. You enjoyed your land, gardens, animals, art, photography, and your four children. Still, I felt bad about asking so much of you.

I thought I would be happy if I managed to get rid of everything, so that my sons would know I could no longer do any business for them or give them any more money or property, and I wished my relationships with my family were not about money. I just wanted my children and grandchildren to visit me.

Memorial

When her memory loss began, my mother wrote,

> *My greatest frustration is my inability to remember names, phone numbers, addresses—my loss of language skills when I'm trying to talk scares me. ... I can no longer add and subtract or multiply. ... I am having trouble focusing. I forget what I need to take care of. I'm afraid of losing my keys to the car and to my apartment. I no longer want to make decisions or be responsible for all the family papers ... I have lots of fears.*

Like my brothers, I didn't grasp the extent of her fear. How could I? Our mother had always been so strong—a giantess. She said she would outlive us. And I believed, on some primal, childish level, that she would.

Up until then, my mother always kept her letters and journal pages organized, sorted by year and date, and stuffed in large manila envelopes. As I sift through the pile of paper scraps on my lap—disorganized emails and letters from 1999-2002 that she cut into random shapes and stacked on bookshelves—sadness pushes me down like a stone into the seat of my chair. A part of me doesn't want to read these pages because they mark the speed at which her mind deteriorated. The other part wants to understand.

There's a progression. During the onset of her disease, she cut off only the white space at the top and bottom of the pages. Later, her scissors arced in broad ovals, cutting off ends of sentences. Sometimes she scissored out the white space between paragraphs, so that pages hang together by thin threads of sentence fragments. Later still, she removed all the space between paragraphs and then taped the pieces back together.

As I sit here trying to sort these scraps into chronological order, I wonder what she was thinking as she cut them. Did she think she was saving paper by cutting off the margins?

The result is that most emails have no beginning and no end, as though her life was one long narrative, one long call and response between her and her unseen readers on the other end.

When I gave her a Windows PC for Christmas in '99 (I couldn't believe she was still using that vintage 1985, IBM Dos PC), she had such a hard time learning the new system that I wished I'd never bought it for her. When she finally figured out how to use it, she switched from writing letters to sending email because it was easier, instant, and—best of all—free. Regardless of who was on the receiving end, she wrote the same stories she'd been telling for forty or fifty years, rehashing her life, her accomplishments, her fears and opinions about her children.

But the pages in my lap recount these stories with increased urgency, whole lifetimes condensed into a few paragraphs. The story she told and wrote most often—about feeling unwanted by her depressed mother—became so abbreviated, it was like Morse code.

The voice in my head—I was three—was, "bad girl, bad girl, go to Grandma's." Grandma would pick me up, rock me, and say, "Everything will come out in the wash."

It's the story I was most tired of hearing, the one I'd stopped listening to years ago, and the one that now gives me the most pain as I read it afresh in email after email. It's like watching my mother fold back into herself all over again, into that three-year-old child waiting for everything in life to be washed clean. And I suppose, in a horrible way, it was.

Now, I'm grateful she wrote the history of her childhood in such concise, easy-to-digest snippets. And I understand, finally, her nostalgia for the large, extended family of her childhood.

> As a child, I was close to all members of the family. I spent a lot of time with my grandmothers and loved being part of both families. Grandma Corker spoiled us all. Grandma Kreiss was the one we lived with when I was born. ... We were a family of fifty or more people for Christmas, Thanksgiving, summer vacations, and time together... Now that my cousin Betty just died, I am the only living Corker with these kinds of memories.

She filled her emails with news of her children: our love lives, personal problems, work—including how much money we made, whether or not she thought we were good parents, and opinions about our characters and those of our children. The worst part, for me, was that her information was usually inaccurate, exaggerated, or downright wrong. When I had my software business, she wrote, "Linda makes $100,000 a year. She has an attorney, an accountant, the insurance, the retirement, and the anxiety." The only true part was the anxiety. When I moved to the Sierra Foothills, she wrote, "Linda and her family are vegetarians. They eat only vegetables grown on their own land." I was a vegetarian, but my children weren't, and we shopped for our food at the local grocery store. I tried not to let her emails rankle me, but they did: whose business was it how much money I made or what my family and I ate?

But once something lodged in her head a certain way, there was no changing it. As her memory worsened, the exaggerations and inaccuracies also became more negative. It wouldn't have bothered me so much if she hadn't sent those emails to everyone—family, friends, and acquaintances alike. With email, she had the power of unlimited, virtual carbon copies at the tips of her fingers.

"Take it with a grain of salt," I'd tell myself.

She knew I hated the way she broadcast her version of my life to the world, but that never stopped her: *Why do you care what anyone else thinks?*

I am the one stopped now, by a paragraph journaled in May of 2001:

> *Each of the six kids of mine has certain positive qualities which I recognize. I focus on their weaknesses out of fear, which doesn't help or change anything.*

I'm surprised. I thought she wasn't aware of her negativity or the pain it caused. How might things have been different if she'd acknowledged our positive traits—to our faces? If she had broadcast our successes instead of our failures, had balanced her public narrative of our lives. Would I have felt more accepted and loved? Would I have wanted to share my thoughts with her, instead of keeping them to myself for fear of how they'd appear in her letters to others?

In these carefully carved emails I hold, she told everyone she had *brain damage. In our family,* she wrote, *we do not have a dementia or Alzheimer's gene.* I understand why she clung to the idea that her memory loss was brain damage: damage could not be undone, but it would not get any worse; she would remain in control of her life and death. At an intuitive, gut level—and later, after the Alzheimer's diagnosis, which she hid from us—she must have known otherwise. But I believed her when I first read these words years ago.

Now, I see the injustice of my anger toward my brothers when they refused to acknowledge her incompetence; I was just as blind. I wanted to believe, as much as they did, that her problems were the temporary results of anxiety.

In one journal entry, she wondered how to find a doctor who would cooperate with assisted suicide, and grappled with the problem of knowing when to end her life:

I have to be aware of when a doctor will proclaim that I am no longer of sound mind. When that day comes, or that phrase, I will no longer have the right to decide when my time is up.

Time and distance allow for the clearest views. I see only now how the incessant writing and repetition of stories was her attempt to hold onto her mind. If I had only seen my mother clearly and not through my own defenses, I might have understood: As long as she had memories, she had life. For her, everything came down to keeping those memories alive.

On May 6, 2007, there were no more letters or journals. No more memories. Alzheimer's had silenced my mother, and she was dying. She had forgotten how to swallow, was no longer able to eat or drink, and it was only a matter of time before her struggle would come to an end. The weight of caring for her would soon lift from me, and my life would return to normal, though I was no longer sure what I meant by *normal*.

I rolled her bed close to the sliding glass door leading from her bedroom to the Berkshire's courtyard and cracked open the vertical blinds. Filtered light fell across her face in thin ribbons. In sleep, her eyes moved beneath the veil of her eyelids, the fingers of her hands twitched, and blue vein rivulets pulsed delicately under the parchment of her skin. I gazed around the dim room, at its beige carpet and institutional off-white walls, and wished for some other ending, one fitting the unconventional, adventurous life she'd led. Not this dreary, drawn out, fading away.

The night before, I had awakened gasping from a dream in which I'd been inside my mother's skin, fighting for breath, suffocating, terrified. I couldn't sleep for a long time afterwards. I lay in bed thinking about all the years I'd fought against her, all the years the Tar prevented me from seeing her clearly. And though I had, over time, begun to view her with more compassion, the thick, gooey stuff remained. I had the idea that if I could be present when she breathed her last, our wounds would be magically healed and the burden of muddy Tar would be washed away.

That afternoon, Michael and David arrived, along with David's wife and children. My mother was breathing heavily, making an automated pumping sound as if she were hooked up to a respirator. David walked to the bed and placed his hand over hers.

"I think Mom's blind," I said. "Her eyes are clouded over, and they aren't tracking moving objects."

David said, "Are you sure? Because she just followed my hand movement."

I got up from the chair where I'd been keeping vigil and went to see for myself. My mother's eyes were wide open and clear, and she seemed to be focusing on David. "See?" he said. While we stood looking down at her, she exhaled one last time and went still, and it seemed to me that she had been waiting for the three of us—the three of us—to be together with her in the room. As if somehow she knew that John would not come, and that Terry and Richard could not be there.

I was by her side for that last breath, but there was no magic removal of the past. Everything was as before, only now I felt the Tar as a dull, thick pain in my chest. Michael held me as I sobbed against his shoulder, and after I was done crying, we stood beside the bed, watching our mother's skin fade from pink to a smooth alabaster.

She was beautiful.

We brought chairs next to the bed and sat beside her for a while, reminiscing, joking about how she used to save and reuse everything— even paper towels, hanging them to dry and using them again until they fell apart. One of the Berkshire staff came into the room and told us it was "root beer float day" and asked if we wanted any. We said yes. And so it happened that we sat around my mother's deathbed laughing and drinking root beer floats. I wondered what the Berkshire staff thought about us, but then I heard my mother's voice in my mind: *Why do you care what anyone else thinks?* And I smiled.

Because my mother had donated her body to science, there wasn't a funeral or a gravesite or an urn filled with ashes. She was gone in every sense of the word. In the weeks after her death, I'd find myself unaccountably parked in front of the Berkshire, or driving down its street, not knowing how I'd gotten there. I thought her death would be a relief. I thought I'd already grieved her passing as she faded away. But I was wrong. My life felt too open, too empty, purposeless without the constant responsibility of her care.

I needed a memorial.

I set a date, reserved a room at the Marriott, and made arrangements for flowers and catered hors d'oeuvres. I invited our relatives and put a notice in the paper. I spent days poring over photo albums and scanning pictures of my mother in every phase of life, from her first baby picture to her last photo before we moved her to assisted living. I created a slide show with soft piano music and put it on DVD. Then I made a book and ordered five copies—one for my mother's sister and brother, and one each for Michael, David, and me. I enlarged, printed, and framed several photographs; the largest would stand on an easel at the front of the room. Finally, I wrote a eulogy. Each of these activities restored my sense of purpose.

But guilt for spending my mother's money on her own memorial dogged me. I thought she'd be rolling over in her grave—if she'd had one—to see me "wasting" her money that way. In talking about arrangements for after her death, she'd once told me one of the motivations for donating her body to research was to save the cost of a funeral. Here I was, spending it anyway.

On the day of the memorial, I worried that no one would show up, I'd not be able to read the eulogy, or the slide show wouldn't work. I arrived early at the hotel, supervised the arrangement of tables and chairs and flowers, checked the slide show—twice—and paced up and down the hallway practicing the eulogy.

More than forty people showed up, including relatives I didn't even know I had, and friends of my mother's who'd seen the memorial notice in the paper. As I looked around at everyone, I recalled the day we gathered in the community clubhouse for her bon voyage party, how proud and happy my mother had been, and felt satisfied with my decision to go ahead with the memorial.

The slide show made us all cry. I invited anyone who wanted to speak about my mother to do so. My mother's brother, my uncle Mike, got up and talked lovingly about his big sister Jackie, who was twenty-two when he was born. My brother Michael spoke about how Mom loved to travel, taking us with her around the world and flying a small plane all over the States and South America.

When he was done, David said, "I never knew the woman you've all been talking about. I didn't know my mother when she was younger, when she traveled around the world or flew a small plane. I didn't know her as a teacher or as someone with all these achievements. The woman you describe is not the mother I remember, but I will miss her all the same."

David was right. She'd been forty-six when he was born, and by the time he was in his mid-teens, she'd retired from full-time teaching. She'd been a different mother to each of her children, our relationships unique reflections of who she was when it mattered most to each of us.

I thought then that when I eventually read her journals and letters, I needed to remember David's words. Perhaps understanding who she'd been during my formative and young adult years would be the key to understanding the mother she'd been to me. And I hoped that understanding might lead to forgiving, and forgiving to finally dissolving the Tar.

JACKIE

I played life as if it were a race with "winning" as the goal. I won: twenty-five years with one man, several mad love affairs, six children and sixteen grandchildren, two advanced degrees, eight books, and travel around the world. I wanted to be financially secure. I won that race too. I loved winning just as I loved loving—for the feel of it.

You children were the greatest joys and greatest heartaches of my life. The second greatest satisfaction was the accident of having teaching find me. I never thought of being a teacher: it found me, and I always thought I was a better teacher than a mother.

When I had misunderstandings with my children, I believed that our love would conquer and result in forgiveness. In cases where it didn't result in forgiveness (John), I decided I could live with that by honoring his decision to be unforgiving. I always believed that before the end John's capacity to forgive would win. I was wrong, but while I waited for John, it helped to know that five out of six had the great gift of forgiveness.

I always believed this life is all there is—death is a cessation of being. Once we die we no longer experience anything, because we don't have a brain or a sensory system. And we don't have another life. This, then, is our only opportunity to be and do whatever it is we can. To live each day as if it were the last and as if we could live forever, is to make the most of life.

A time came when I felt I had been everywhere, done everything, and met everybody. Then I knew having everything I wanted was not what life's about. For me, life was the climb—the intensity, the energy, the aliveness, the excitement of wanting something new and going for it. I was a native Californian pioneer always searching for another horizon—something new and different. I still wanted to Go West.

Final Words

My heart leaps with surprise and pleasure when I discover the journal entry, with the year *1975* scrawled, like an afterthought, in my mother's handwriting across the top of the page:

> *When I die, I would like my family to have a goodbye party with bal-loons and games and pictures and holding hands and crying and laughing and sharing the best memories and forgetting the worst—a ceremony of love and forgiveness and letting go.*

> *While we physically die, our family relationships live on as long as there is one person who lives with the memory of that relationship. While we fear a prolonged period of dying, the experience of death may unite a family again and provide us momentarily with the meaning of life—the capacity to love.*

It's been more than five years since the memorial, and more than four since I brought home my mother's little brown diary. As I read, I think about the slideshow and the pictures of my mother placed around the room; the party afterwards with everyone crying and laughing as they shared their memories of Jackie; the food; the children and grand-children and cousins wrestling on the lawn in the hotel's courtyard. We didn't have balloons, but we had everything else.

Reading my mother's letters and journals has made me realize the ways I have been like her: divorced twice, I had four children over a space of nineteen years, and I sometimes overlooked their emotional needs while seeking to meet my own, eventually finding satisfaction as a teacher and writer. Now, only after realizing how much I am like her can I appreciate the ways I am different: I don't try to control my children; I don't demand that they phone, or write, or do anything for me they don't want to; I know how to keep secrets; I have no need for anxiety's adrenaline rush; and yes, I do care how others feel and what they think.

Reading her versions of our life did not dissolve the Tar as I'd hoped. I do not find myself awash with forgiveness or a healing sense of closure. But there's something different about the Tar's quality—it's less viscous, more fluid, more dishwater gray than black. The Tar that remains, stained into my being, is less like anger and hatred, more like sadness and regret, a feeling of too little too late, a wish that I'd understood her better while she was present.

I'm grateful she left the treasure chest of her perceptions and memories behind for me to read. The woman I found in the pages of her letters and journals was not the mother I thought I'd lost. Neither was she—as David put it—the mother I remember. Jackie was an extraordinary, complicated, and passionate woman, who did all that any of us ever do—the best she knew how. And I think I might be able—finally—to let her Go West.

Appendix

Obituary, written by Jackie, 1998

<u>OBITUARY</u>

Jacquelyn B. Carr sums up her life: "I lived three lives for the price of three. I paid my dues and reaped my rewards." Born in 1923 to young, uneducated parents, Jackie Corker entered school in Oakland. In 1929 during the Great Depression, when her father lost his job, this six year old watched as the family car was repossessed, two men in a truck took all the furniture, then Jackie remembers sleeping on a couch in "someone's" house until her father found a job as a gardener in San Francisco. As an adult, Jackie said, "My first motivation in life was to be safe - which meant to own a house so that it couldn't be taken away."

Eventually the family moved back to Oakland where 'Jackie' graduated 12th highest in her class at University High School in North Oakland. In spite of her mother's comment, "Girls don't go to college", Jackie entered U.C. Berkeley, married her high school sweetheart, and earned an A.A. degree before her first son was born. During World War II., while her husband spent three years in the U.S.Air Force, Jackie, took her baby with her and worked as a cook for a family that paid $150 per month, room, and meals. She bought a bicycle, put her son in the basket, and biked to a school that paid her $100. a month. Her army allot- ment was $60. At age 22, she paid cash for her first house in Tomales Bay and boarded children until W.W.II was over.

After her husband returned from overseas, the family moved back to Oakland. As the family grew, Jackie continued buying real estate until she owned 2 houses, 14 units, and a hotel. In between children and real estate, she continued her education until she had a four year degree from U.C.Berkeley, a California State teaching credential and a teaching contract at Hillsdale High School in San Mateo. After 11 years of teaching and 22 years of marriage, Jackie divorced, sold the house and posses- sions; and as a single mother took her children around the world for 365 days. When they returned, she bought a 180 Piper Chero- kee, and during summer vacation, she flew with her children 48 states, Bahamas, and Canada. The following summer they flew the rim of South America, island hopped the Caribbean to Miami, then flew back to California where she sold '99 Juliet.

Before Jackie started teaching at Foothill College in 1969, she earned a masters at Stanford. By 1973, she had completed her PhD from University of Southern California followed by publishing many books, some into third editions. In 1984, she donated $25,000. to Foothill College, bought computers and printers, and set up a computer center in the Language Arts Division. She taught 14 different courses in four departments: English, Speech, Psychology, and Word Processing. She created and taught Communi- ty Courses, conducted workshops for the U.S. Air Force and many Silicon Valley companies in addition to her volunteer work. In 1986, Jackie donated a house to the National Environmental Asso- ciation. In 1992, she donated a house to Stanford. This matri- arch who headed a family of 26, said, "My goal is to give it all away before I die." And She Did!

Sketch by Whitney Cushing, Florida artist

Travel Records

TRAVEL } 50 - U. S. States (*many more than once*)
112 - Foreign Countries (*many more than once*)

```
1923-1933 - First 18 years - Neptune Beach, Alameda, San Francisco,
            Santa Cruz; Forest Hill - Uncle Charlie,
1935/36 - Camp Wasibo, Santa Cruz Mts. (Camp Fire Girls)
1937 - Sacramento (Uncle Earle), Lower Lake (Aunt Myrtle)
1939 - Treasure Island, Golden Gate Exposition, World's Fair
1940 - Marsh Creek (Jack), Russian River, Photo Contest,
1941 - December - Mexico with Alice Cordero
1942 - April 3rd - Carson City, Nevada (married Jack)
       Summer - Pinecrest
1943 - W.W.II - Following Jack - Fresno, Amarillo, Texas;
1943 - To meet Jack before he went overseas - Denver, Colorado
1945 - I worked at Tahoe (Terry with me); Tomales Bay House,
1947 - With Jack; Catalina Island, Lake Tahoe,
1949 - Jack & I drove 6,000 miles across U.S. Jack and I were
       26, Terry 6, John 2 (3 days going, 9 days visit, 5 back.
1950 - Worked in Reno, Summer - Richard from U.C. Berkeley
       Honeymoon Apts., Santa Cruz, Sept. - State Fair
1951 - January - U.C. Lodge (snow)
1952 - July - Yosemite
1953 - Feb. - Cal Ski Lodge; Summer - State Fair
1954 - Snow trip, May - Carmel (Wheeler); Marsh Creek, Big Basin
1955 - Palm's Hotel - Golden Gate Park/S.F.Zoo on Sunday's off.
1956 - January - to Las Vegas (Dad/Helene marrie)
1963 - Jack and I went to Europe for 5 weeks on a tour      } 17
       (Amsterdam, Germany, Austria, Venice, Florence, Naples, Blue
       Grotto, Capri, Rome, Milan, Lucerne, Geneva, Paris, Calais,
       Dover, London, New York, N.J., Maryland, Wash. D.C., Mt. Vernon,
       (Reno, Nevada - Divorce)
1964 - Spring - Acapulco (Fish, James Carrigan Jr. III) & Mexico City > 1
       Lake Co. (ED.)  December - Death VAlley, Arizona
1965-66 - N.Y. World Fair, Around the World (Linda & Mike) John -] 60
          first half,  Richard met us in Japan,  (Bill Brickner) ]
1966 - Monterey (Armond Wilson);
       Alaska (Bill Brickner)Juneau; Fairbanks; Victoria, Canada > 1
       Yosemite (VW CAmper), Esalen,
       I learned to fly - La Jolla, Solvang, California, Oregon,
       Nevada,
1967 - Flew 48 States, Bahamas & Canada in '99er Juliet  > 1
       my 180, single engine, Cherokee - four seat'er
       (Joe Beard & Bill Brickner)
       December - Acapulco with Volney Bell; Las Vegas,
       Santa Barbara; San Francisco
1968 - Easter - Tahiti, Moorea, Bora Bora,  (Married Bill Wilson)} 3
       Summer flight with Mike around South America.
1969 - David Born January 12th.  Flew with him to Los Angeles to } 22
       Terry/Wendy wedding
1970 - March - Flew to St. Louis, Miss. (Took David to see
       Grandparents).  Flew to New York to see publisher
       June 30: (David - 17 months)
       San Francisco to Honolulu, Pago Pago (American
       Samoa), Nandi (Fiji, New Zealand, Aukland (New   } Took
       Zealand) 3 day tour of the south; stayed with family / David  5
       Sydney, Australia; (3 day bus to Canberra, Melbourne/
```

1

```
          back to Sydney; David got sick; rush to get home.
          Australia, To Hawaii, to San Francisco July 24th
          28 hrs.  Across equator & International date line
          August - Bill's parents came to Redwood City to visit.
          Bought cabin in La Honda
1971 & 72 - Los Angeles - PhD Program; David in day care
1973 - Phd.; Embarcadero party; (Ross) (Wayne Knapp)
1974 - Sleepy Hollow Motel, Tahoe; Rick/LuAnn;
1975 - Stanford St. (Lee Bishop)
          Lincoln City, Oregon to Visit Linda/Eric
          Dec. flew to Goshen, Indiana - Heather born;
1976 - June flight to Portland - Ezra Born; David 7 1/2 yrs.
          Summer - Flew to Oaklahoma (Albert Kelly ranch)
                   Flew to Florida (George Cone) Kennedy Space
                   Center, Florida Disneyland - Return Greyhound Bus
          August - Greyhound - Portland with David
          December - Disneyland and Tahoe
1977 - Sacramento - Roy from Sacramento area
          December - Hawaii with David & John
1978 - Spring - Yucatan, Mexico; Havana, Cuba (Hemingway)
          May Portland - Evan Born; David 9 yrs.
          June - Susanville State Prison - Mike
          Summer in Europe (Jerry); Terry in Paris
          August - Picked up Heather in Vancouver
1979 - Easter - Vancouver, Wash.
          Summer - Took David Across Canada - Amtrak Super-Liner
                   (Bamff, Lake Louise) Greyhound back
                   Ferry to Victoria - Ship to Seattle
          December - Heather/Rick/David to Hearst Castle, L.A.
                   Tiajuana, Disneyland(3rd time for David)
                   Universal STudios, Marineland, Catalina Island
1980 - Dottie Died; Heather came to live with me; Bill Wilson
          visit at the Cabin; Thanksgiving - Portland - Bought
          Marshall St. - December bought Burnside
          Christmas - Amtrak to L.A.
1981 - March - Sun River, Oregon (Heather); Portland
          Spring - Pinnacles Nation'l Monument; San Juan Batista,
                   Santa Cruz Light House, RailFair - Sacramento
          Summer - David & I drove 9600 Miles of U.S. - Youth Hostels
                   31 States, National Parks/Monuments, Wilsons in
                   St. Louise, Wash. D.C. and return
          December - Christmas - 2 weeks (Bill & Elzie Wilson)
1982 - Several Portland Trips -
1983 - January - Ano Nuevo - Elephant Seals
          February - Silverado, Napa - my 60th B'day party at Bev's
          March - Santa Cruz with David
          May - mother's day all day passes on Board Walk
                   Sacramento, Delta (Stanley's boat)
          June - Portland, Canada, Victoria, with David
                   Family Camp in Coos Bay (took Heather)
                   L.A. - Terry/Chika (Dec. Rick/Family move to CA.)
1984 - Even/Ezra/Heather to Terry's, Disneyland (Youth Hostel)
          Computer conference - Ogden, Utah
          June - Mike's Wedding; Linda/Eric to Europe (Computer Lab)
          Bill Pabst moved in to Share Stanford house
```

1985 - David 16 - boy'sranch; I Retired; *(First time)*
          Linda/Eric/Ezra/Evan moved in - Bill out
          Holloman Air Force Base, New Mexico (I gave two wrkshops)
1986 - Linda fam. moved to Mt. View house;
          Brigham Young University - Utah - genealogy conference
          August - Feather River - Elderhostel (Bob Jennings);
          Last trip to Burnside; Portland; Expo '86 -
    Vancouver, Canada, World's Fair;
          Aug. 31 - Bev's belated birthday party - Cabin
          November - Sacramento (Bill/Bev/Ed) Terry's Movie

1987 - Drove to Terry's; then to Tiajuana; Guaymus (Millie/Russ)
                              (9th)
1988 - David's birthday - Helicopter ride over San Francisco
          Richard, kids and I went to Lake County to visit John

1990 - June 30 - Disney Land; David, Rayna, Jenny, Taylor

1991 - Zen Center - Marin Co. (Elderhostel)

1992 - July - Mensa Conference (4 days)
          August - Visited Milli and Russ (Sugar Pine)
          Oct. - Inez's 90th B'day Party - Kreiss Family

1993 - May - Visit Cousin Betty - Fresno overnite
          Sheno Retreat Center - North of S.Francisco (Elderhostel)
          July - Wilber's 80th B'day - Kreiss Family
          September - Asilomar Mensa Weekend
          October - Mensa Santa Cruz (KOA Camp-cabin) With Jenny
          November - Disney Land/Univ. Studios/Magic Mt.
                        Mike and three girls
          Dec. - Puerta Vajarta/Lake Chapala; Mexico (With Mike)
                  (Visit Richard)

1994 - Aug. Mt. Madana, Santa Cruz (Elderhostel)
          Kotani-En - Classical Japanese Gardens - Monte Serena
          Mt. Madan - Appointment with Babaji;
          December 14 - Aidan Born

1995 - Dec. - Portland - Rick in jail;
              Brought Heather Back to live with me.

1996 - San Francisco Health Seminar (Elderhostel)
          April 8 - Arieka Born; I flew to Los Angeles
          Retired Foothill - Applied for U.S.Peace Corps. *(Retired again)*

1997 - Sri Lanka - United State Peace Corps. (April 30 - Nov. 30)
          May 18 - Going Away Party
          May 29 - U.S.Peace Corps - San Francisco
          June 1 - 1 A.M. Land in Colombo _(Sri Lanka) _____ ↓
              Culture Shock - Disappointment, fear, stress,
          June 5-19 - Negumbo - Teacher's Training College
          June 21-August 19 - Live in Poddala Village (with Family)
              Teaching - Narawala Elementary Sch.
          Training includes travel through Sri Lanka

3

```
July 21 - Travelers nest - Kandy
Fall - 9 days in Colombo Hospital
        head injury (6 stitches), cracked ribs, whip lash
August 6 - Climbed Sigiriya Rock Fortress - 1,200 steps
August 22, Swearing In Ceremony Colombo
August 26 - Peredenia - English Teacher's College
        (Chitra. daughter and son)
Sept. 26th - University of Peradeniya
    Marrs Hill: Gunaratne Family (2 sons, 1 daughter)
October 27th - Tamil's Bomb Columbo;  I am in Colombo
        Emergency Evacuation training on Island
    "Conditions Beyond your control"  end service
November 30th - Landed in San Francisco - HOME!
December - Moved into Campbell duplex - HOME!

1998 - April - Fly to Los Angeles - Arieka's 2nd Birthday
    Disneyland - Took Mitchell and brother Steven
    August 7, 1998 - Moved into Valley Village
    Tech Museum - Took Jenny and Michell (Bought Membership)
    November - Thanksgiving at Linda's in "Cool!"

1999 - January - Bev/Ed/brother Michael, Aunt Ruth visit/lunch
    April - Flew to Los Angeles - Arieka's birthday
    May - Took Mike/Angel/Steven;Michell/Steven2 to Roaring
        Camp and Big Trees - Narrow-Gauge Railroad
```

June - U.C. Berkley International house Elephant Program
Summer - Took Aidan to California History museum
        Took Steven to " to Tech Museum "
        Took Aidan + Michelle / Mellisa to Tech museum
        and Jenny / michelle / mellisa to Tech museum
October or _Robin Andrews_ - Mike drove me to Vancover, Wash.
November - to see Richard + Cat, Taylor, Rayna, etc.
Thanksgiving > Vally Village - Linda, Jenny, Aiden, Evan, + Sabrina
Christmas - Mike drove me to visit my sister } Bev + Ed.
        Then we drove to Linda's   } Jenny, Aiden } 3 kids +
            "Cool"   } Evan, Sabrina } lots of
                                      } Linda, Mike + me } grandchildren

Friends & Lovers

Friends & Lovers

1. *Matthew*
2. *Helga*
— *Linda*

Men in My Life

1923 — My father, uncles, cousins, neighbor boys

1928 — Kindergarden (twins in my class)

First Date → 1932 — 9 yrs. old — 3rd Grade, San Francisco,
Boy invited me to a Saturday matinee

1935–37 — Grades 6–8; parties, boys in classes, neighbors
Stanyan St. —

1938 — 9th Grade — Howard Oxenham (dates for 4 years, after WWII

1939 — 1941 Grades 10 through 12; 16 to 18 yrs.

Jack Carr, (other boys in school thought I was his girl)
Jack Banker, Kenny Voget, Ivan Owen
Quaker Church: Don, Jimmy Martin, Larry, Lou, Charles
Boys at theatre: Warren Dobson, Bill Marsh, Bud Dooley

1941 — 18 yrs. old — First Year in College — *Brother Mike Born Sept.*
Adams Springs Resport — 3 boys in band, owner's son (Don)
Mexico with Alice — her cousins
U.C. students: Jimmie Treadwell, 3 blind dates,

★ 1942 — Married Jack Carr (both of us were virgins) *Jerry, John, Ricky, Mike*

1944 — (Jack Overseas) *June* 21 yrs. old — I worked at army hospital
18 yr. old serviceman — orderly at the hospital

1948 — Whitey (met at dance)
Jimmie Treadwell — from college (both of us real estate agents)

1950 — Blakes Restaurant — Richard (Dick) Jewish; spring, summer,
at Tahoe, summer '51 in Los Angeles

1953 — Berkeley Police Dept.: Bob, Paul, Ronnie,

★ 1953 — November (30 yrs. old) Deputy Sheriff — John Wheeler *Linda*

1960 — 64 Hillsdale Hi — Ed (math teacher)
Bill Snyder (art teacher)

1962 — Stanford Fellowship (summer) Bernard Della Santina
(Barnie) (Met in Athens in 1965)

DIVORCE — 1963

1964 — Met at Dottie's — Armond Wilson (Black)
1964, 1966, 1970 (New York)

1964–65 Jim Carrigan Jr. III (Spring in Acapulco)

1964 — Royce Hopkins (Manager of the Thunderbird)

1

1964-65 - Paul Montez (Dance Instructor), Tom Tuttle, Bob Singer,

1964-69 - Bill Brickner (Europe, N. Africa, Alaska, Bahamas)

1965 - Bob Parenti

1965-1966 = Trip Around the World

June - London, Maurice Mann, painter

July - Copenhagen - Bob (Commercial Airplane Sales)

August - Stockholm camp grounds - Chuck (played with kids)
         Bernt - Swedish Drummer - Bromma Hotel-Restaurant
         Tod Bohlin (about 65) - met at Drottinghoms Theatre

October - Barcelona - Herbert (German on way to Mexico)
          Jerry from L.A. (Circled Spain, Tangiers, Portugal,

December - Athens (Barney from home)
           Istanbul - Celso Bogado - musician
                      Dave Collins - U.S. Marine Officer

January - Cairo - Blond Egyptian Guide

        - Katmandu - Jewish Israelite Engineer

February - Tokyo -

         U. S. Airforce Captain on leave from Vietnam

March - Bob Hooper, U.S. Capt. 8 days leave from Alaska (Nikko)

        Mr. Miyao - Japanese (25 yrs. old) hires me to teach

      - Saigon - Alan; Australian Engineer

April - Osaka - Alan

      - Tokyo - Gerry Landry (U.S.Paratroopers)
                Warren Houck (Jake) - Zoology Professor, Humboldt
                                      State, California

1966 - Esalen - Psychiatrist of Los Angeles

FLYING - 1966-68

1966 - Ben Trotter, Cessna owner and instructor
1967 - Feb.-March Jerry Landry
1967 - Spring - Joe Beard (Mexico), Summer around U.S.

1967 - Summer Flight Around U.S. (Joe and Bill Brickner)

2

1967 — Volney Bell (20 yrs.); San Francisco Escort Service
             Acapulco, Las Vegas, Santa Barbara, Escondido

   Fall — <u>Ad in Berkeley Barb</u> (Met 35 men)
             (first Ad — once a year)

         Bob Longwish, Captain — TWA Pilot
         Skyler — Bonanza owner

1968 — Bill Wilson (married June, Divorced Nov)   — David

     Summer So. America: Raoul Fabres, Santiago, Chile

1969 — Foothill College: Stan Rosenberry, Jack Hasling,
                         Bill Tinsley
         Phil Hertwick (Hoover St., Redwood City)

1970 — 72 Oregon Green: Mario Rabinowitz, Walt Pollock,
                    Ed Conners, Ross Walker

1972 — 1974 Embarcadero — Ross Walker,
           Jim Craig (Berkeley) Tony Fetisoff (Insurance)
           Wayne Knapp, Fred Mänzel,

1975 — 1984 Stanford Ave., Palo Alto

David Lynch 1975 — Summer — Lee Bishop,·
              Christmas — Alan Newkirk (Met in 1984)

   19.
        1977 summer — Roy (from Sacramento)
   197——   Sept. — Bill (SRI—College Terrace)——————————→ *Herpes*
              Stanley Towle, Willard Holden,
              Ross Nickols (Deck/steps), Bob Boyer,

        1978 — Summer Jerry Seehauf (Europe),   *1*

        1979 — Sarge, Marvin Kahan, Bill Brothers
              Tom Luck (Black)

DAVID 10 1980 — Summer — Bill Wilson Came to California   *2*
        1981 —   " & Winter — to St. Lewis to Bill's

David 12 1982 — 83 — Trellis Ad — Met 25; second date — 12
        " (July bought computer —→moved into single bed)
           Spring '83 — Stanford Conf. — Jim Zellerbach (28 yrs.)
           Pat Milligan, (Bankrupt CPA)   *3*
           Texas — we went to Los Gatos   *4*

        1984 — Trellis Ad (met 20; second date 10)

                      John Agnew, Carl, Stanley, Sarge
              "   November — Bill Pabst shared House First Time

        1986 —   Mensa Computer Tech. from Hayward   *5*
              "   May — Bill Pabst Moved in second time

                              3

<u>REAL ESTATE</u>

1 — 1944 — 5 acres Walnut Creek — Carrs-Corkers-Winthers

2 — 1945 — Tomales Bay

3 — 1946 — 902 60th St. Oakland

4 — 1947 — 6060 Thornhill Dr. Oak.

5 — 1948 — 7112 Snake Rd. Oak.

6 — 1949 — Lot in Lafayette

7 — 1951 (May) — 4535 Walnut St. Oak.

8 — 1953 (May) — 562 Walla Vista, Oak.

9 — 1954 (Dec.) — Fourplex, Oakland

    1955 (Jan.) — Leased Palm's Hotel — Central Ave. Alameda

                Bought back Walla Vista and Resold it.

10 1955 — Seven Units, Alameda

11 1956 (Aug.) — 14 units Vernon/Santa Rosa, Oakland
                 (traded 7 units + 2nd on Dad's House + Cash)

12 1957 (Jan) — 1324 Dayton Ave, Alameda

13 1958 — #1 Ronada, Oakland (Discounted second default)
         Sold side lot to builder

14 1958 (Sept.) — 1728 Lexington, Eichler Highlands, San Mateo

15 1959 — 1320 Yew St., San Mateo
         Sold back lot to neighbor

    1966 — Rented 3611 Page St. Redwood City
    1967 —   "   906 King St. R.C.

16 1969 — 3118 Hoover St. (Duplex), Redwood City

17 1970 — Woodwardia Lodge, 40 acres, La Honda

18 1972 — 2450-11 W. Bayshore, Oregon-Green Condos, Palo Alto

19 1974 — 425-427 Embarcadero Rd., Palo Alto

20 1974 — Sleepy Hollow Motel, Tahoe

21 1975 — 1655 Stanford Ave., Palo Alto

22 1980 — 2365 N.W. Marshall St. — 7 Unit Conversion, Portland, Ore

1

23   1980 - 11833 E. Burnside; Portland, Ore.

Repossessions:

Sold Walla Vista Twice
Sold Yew St. twice + lot
Sold 14 units twice
Sold Sleepy Hollow 3 times: Routery, R.E. Agent, Attorneys
Sold Marshall St. twice (vandalism)
Newon St - (handwritten)
Fire: Burnside (vandalism)

Law Suits: 1 - 60th St. House - Right of way condemnation
            2 - Sleepy Hollow Motel, Tahoe - Fraud suit
            3 - Burnside condemnation/corner by state
            4. Sleepy Hollow (handwritten)

2

WORK HISTORY

age

11 - 1934 - Sold cookies for Camp Fire Girls (earned camp)
Sold pies
baby-sitting

16 - 1939 - Housecleaning for neighbors (Lelbach's)
Library assistant - University High School
Sales girl - Withorn & Swan's Dept. Store
Theatrical employees union: Usherette: Fox Calif.Thtr.
(.25 cents per hr.)

18 - 1941 - Cannery workers union
Modeling Contest - $5. per hr.
Waitress: Adam's Springs Summer Resort
Waitress: Berkeley Inn, Whitecotton Hotel
Cashier - Berkeley Theater

19 - 1942 - Cashier/Bookkeeper/Payroll - Alameda Theater

20 - 1943 - Baby-sitter, housework - Amarillo Texas

21 - 1944 - Household Live-In - Woodside Family
Cook (Live-In) - Carr Family, Palo Alto, CA.
Teaching Assistant - Educ. Guidance Center:
Private School, P.A.

22 - 1945 - Emergency Calif. Teach. Credential: substitute -4th gr.
Nurse's Aide: U.S. Army Hospital, Oakland (nights)
Practical Nurse: Nurses Registry of Alameda Co.
Real Estate: Acreage, First house-Tomales Bay
Typist/Office Work - Tahoe
Licensed Forest/Parent Home Care - Tomales Bay
Sales: Childcraft Corp.
Nursery School assistant

25 - 1948 - Real Estate License: Stanfield Realty

26 - 1949 - Ironing (out of my home)
Sold first article - Family Circle ($5.)
County License - child care: Boarded Family

27 - 1950 - Cashier/Hostess/Bookkeeping: Blake's Restaurant - Berk.
Shill, waitress: Nevada Inn, Reno

28 - 1951 - State Licensed Knitting/Assembling: Private Shop

29 - 1952 - Waitress - Dan's Cafe (Dinner Shift)
Policewoman - Berkeley Police Dept. (Nov.)

30 - 1953 - Reader: Univ. of Cal. Berkeley
Deputy Sheriff: Alameda Co. - Santa Rita
Apartment Owner/Management: 14 units, Oakland

1

31 — 1954 — Resigned Deputy Sheriff Alameda Co.

32 — 1955 — Managed Residential Hotel (50 Rooms) — Palm's Hotel

35 — 1958 — Teacher: Hillsdale High School

37 — 196? — Night Teacher: San Mateo Junior College

42 — 1969 — Instructor: Foothill College

      1980's — Industrial Psychologist
               Executive Secretary at Fairchild

Consulting: Fairchild, EPRI, U.S. Air Force

1986 — Menlo College — Fall quarter Freshman English

Cj ameel — 1989
nat'l — 1991
1990 — Baby sitting — Mother's in Bed

2

PUBLISHING

1949 — Family Circle — $5.00

May 1963 — "Philosophy of Education" Advance Star, Burlingame
              Reproduced by Education Dept. — S.F.State Univ.

March 1964 — "Project Freedom" — The English Journal
              Reproduced by Carl Rogers — On Personal Power

November 1964 — "Senior English — Business Emphasis";
              The English Journal

Nov. 28, 1965 — "Touring the World"; Iberian Times
              Barcelona, Times.

January 1966 — "Around the World: GYPSYWAGON" Small World
              Introduction reproduced and used in
              Palmer's Writers School

July 23, 1966 — "Around the World in a Year";
              San Mateo Times: Week-end Supplement

January 1967 — "Around the World on a Sabbatical"
              Scholastic Teacher

July/August 1967 — "Flight Plan for Fems" Les Gals

Feb./March 1968 — "It Takes All Kinds"; Les Gals

March 1968 — "Flying Educator"; National Business Women

April 1968 — "Airport Hunting in Wyoming"; Plane & Pilot

June 1968 — "Saigon: Vietnam Report"; Les Gals.

Vol.3, #4 — "Crisis: The American Marriage — The Awakening
              Individualist"; Les Gals

Vol.3, #6 — "Crisis: The Short Term Marriage"; Les Gals

November 1970 — "Over To You, Student" An Interview;
              Home Journal, New Zealand

(?)-Lost: "South American Adventure"; Les Gals

1970 — Learning is Living; Exposition/Banner Press, N.Y.

May 1973 — PhD Dissertation: U.S.C.
              Cognitive Bheavior Objectives for General Psychology
              At the Community College.

August 1976 — "It Takes All Kinds" — Reproduced in The Answer

1

1979 — <u>Communicating and Relating</u>: Benjamin Cummings, Menlo Park

1979 — <u>Communicating with Myself: A Journal</u>:
                              Benjamin Cummings, Menlo Park, CA

1984 — <u>Communicating and Relating</u>: Wm. C. Brown, Dubuque, Iowa

1984 — <u>Communicating with Myself: A Journal</u>:
                              Wm. C. Brown, Dubuque, Iowa

1987 — <u>Equal Partners: The Art of Creative Marriage</u>
                              Reed Publishing, Cupertino, CA

1987 — <u>The Crisis in Intimacy</u> (Contract with Brooks-Cole Pub.)

1991 —
3rd Ed.
1991 — 2nd Ed.

2

Acknowledgements

I am deeply grateful for the patient guidance of my advisor and mentor, Lowell Cohn, who helped me uncover and shape the heart of my story and without whom I could not have written this memoir.

I also want to thank the Creative Writing faculty at the University of San Francisco, in particular Stephen Beachy, Kate Moses, and Lewis Buzbee, who suffered through many first drafts of what would eventually become the chapters of this book. And my cohorts in the MFA program, for your honest criticism and encouragement: Nicole Zimmerman, Todd Cincala, LeeAnn Prescott, Savanna Ferguson, Lina Shustarovich, Isabel Choi, and Yolanda Venegas.

To the members of my writing group: Patsy Ann Taylor, Barbara Toboni, and Christina Julian. Thank you for your advice, your faith in me as a writer, and your friendship. I am forever in your debt.

To my brothers, John, Michael, and David: thank you for putting up with my endless questions about our past and helping me to remember.

And to my sweetheart, Rich, for your undying support and love. Without you, I would not have been able to complete this journey.

ABOUT THE AUTHOR

Amber Lea Starfire is the author of *Week by Week: A Year's Worth of Journaling Prompts & Meditations* and co-editor of *Times They Were A-Changing: Women Remember the '60s & '70s*. She earned her MFA in Creative Writing from the University of San Francisco and an MA in Education from Stanford University. Coordinator for the Story Circle Network's Online Classes Program, Amber also teaches creative writing and journaling and works as a freelance editor. Her work has appeared in literary journals and anthologies including *Beyond Boundaries* and *Vintage Voices 2012: Call of the Wild*. She is a member of the California Writers Club, the Story Circle Network, National Association of Memoir Writers (NAMW), and International Association for Journal Writing (IAJW). Visit Amber's website: www.writingthroughlife.com.

Made in the USA
Charleston, SC
06 May 2014

babysat, boarded children, rented rooms—did things you would find "horrifying" to earn a little money.

After I returned from visiting you, John laid into me, telling me everything he didn't like about me: He said everyone was tired of hearing about my book, my work, my boyfriends, my problems around the house. I used people, he said. I talked too much, was too critical, and didn't have any friends because all I cared about was myself, and boyfriends couldn't hang around because I didn't know how to have "real" relationships. He said that none of you needed my help. You didn't need your teeth fixed or your rent paid or your cars fixed or anything, and that you'd all get along fine without me.

The problem was that when I helped, I put all of you in a position of feeling obligated and indebted. So when I needed help, like the lawn mowed or the driveway swept, none of you wanted to do it, and then you felt guilty.

Times like that made being a mother more pain than joy. I could stand it when all of you had problems, but I couldn't stand it when I got that barrage of negative judgments and dislike.

My number one priority in my life was my family. I knew that my strength was a drag for all of you. That I talked too much. That I opened up with everything that came through my mind and heart, and that this was too much for you kids. You really didn't want to hear it all. But I wanted to share it all so I did it anyway. Other than the men in my life, I didn't have the time to spend with other people. Friendship was not important to me because I wanted my children to be my friends. That was a pretty big order, I guess. Probably impossible. But the word "friend" meant nothing to me. I wanted to share my feelings, thoughts, pains, and successes with my children, not with outsiders. Was it too much to ask to share my feelings and thoughts with you kids? I was going to do it anyway—if it drove you away, then that was your choice.